CRUSH DEBT NOW!

Pay Off Debt, Fight Collection Lawsuits, Negotiate And Settle Your Debts Using 3-Step Strategy To Be Debt Free

THOMAS CROMWELL

© Copyright 2020 - All rights reserved.

It is not legal to reproduce, duplicate, or transmit any part of this document in either electronic means or in printed format. Recording of this publication is strictly prohibited and any storage of this document is not allowed unless with written permission from the publisher except for the use of brief quotations in a book review.

DISCLAIMER

This book is produced as is. I make no representations as to the accuracy, completeness, suitability, or validity of anything contained therein. The information in this book represents the opinion of the author, based on experience and research, it must **not** be construed as specific legal or financial advice. You are solely responsible for your legal and financial decisions - please engage your own advisors. Neither the author nor publisher accepts any liability for direct, indirect, or consequential loss or damages howsoever arising from the information provided in this book.

CONTENTS

The Personal Financial Toolkit   v
Introduction   vii

Chapter One: Moving the Debt Mountain   1
Chapter Two: When Creditors Attack   17
Chapter Three: Debt Destruction Strategies   34
Chapter Four: How to Hack Your Loans   49
Chapter Five: Debt management plans   59
Chapter Six: The Secrets of Negotiation That You Must Know   64
Chapter Seven: How to Get What You Want In Just 3 Steps   84
Chapter Eight: Fightback using Repudiation   100
Chapter Nine: Debt Specific Information   115
Chapter Ten: The Nuclear Solution to Debt - How to Blow up Your Debt   129

Final Words   143
Author's note   147
References   149

THE PERSONAL FINANCIAL TOOLKIT

(Never take on your creditors without this)

Smash your goals, save time and effort on your budgets, fight debt collectors: get access to our devastatingly useful financial toolkit:

- Fight creditors and debt collectors with must-have templates
- The Loan Calculator will work out when you will be debt-free
- Track your spending with the budget planner.
- Pre-configured with **21** critical budget categories.
- The visual goal planner will capture and motivate your drive to prosperity.

Get the must-have templates to challenge your creditors and verify your debts. Our loan calculator will allow you to vary the interest rate and payment to tell you the term on a loan.

To receive your **FREE** personal financial toolkit including the amazing loan calculator, must-have templates, and 7 new monster money-saving tips, visit the link:

www.personalfinancewizard.com

INTRODUCTION

Do you have excessive debts with no idea how you will pay them off?

Are you being pursued by your creditors, receiving aggressive phone calls from debt collectors, and letters demanding payment?

Are your lenders threatening you with court action and taking some of your wages?

15% of Americans said that they had been pursued by a debt collector, according to a report by the Consumer Financial Protection bureau in 2017. Only one in four of these attended the court hearing. In all the other cases, it is almost certain the collectors will have benefited from default decisions in their favor. A judgment that would allow the debt collector to receive a percentage of wages or sequester other assets.

If any of these situations apply to you, then this book has been created to provide your solutions. With this book, you will discover how you can deal effectively with these problems and crush your oppressive debts!

By reading this book, you will:

- Understand your debts; how and why they are perpetually draining your health and wealth.
- Find out if your debt is sustainable.
- Learn what to do if your creditors attempt to sequester your assets or wages.
- Understand the legal processes and how to fight or stop the process.
- Learn how to fight debt collections calls.
- Know when not to use loan consolidation and why these are frequently scam attacks.
- Master useful tips on how to negotiate with your creditors - and win!
- Be able to save money on all different types of debt including utilities, taxes, mortgages, rent, vehicle loans, student debt, credit cards, and other loans.
- Know when and how to use nuclear options of bankruptcy and insolvency.

This book has been created to help people with serious and chronic debt problems. It is not aimed at people who are a few thousand dollars in debt who want to pay down their debts and need to manage their budget better and create savings. This is the topic of our first book in the Personal Finance Wizard series "Perpetually Broke: Living Beyond Your Income". "Crush Debt Now" is intended for debtors with unsustainable and severe financial issues, where some or all of the debt is already delinquent.

I have a wealth of practical and commercial finance experience to draw on in writing this series of books on personal finance. I experienced an upbringing that showed me the value of every penny earned or spent, but I also learned that many other people, even those earning good salaries have an uncomfortable relationship with money. I can show you how it is possible to rise, phoenix-like, from almost any situation, however desperate it may seem.

In this book, we will cover practical examples and advice to dramatically reduce the burden of your unsustainable debts, and bring back sanity to your finances. When you follow the step-by-step guide for all types of personal debts, then you can expect to save thousands or even tens of thousands (of dollars) in repayments. You can crush your outstanding debt and be completely free and be financially solvent within two years.

Using the 3-step negotiating strategy in this book is a proven approach for drastic debt reductions for people of all different backgrounds and income levels. The most successful case I have faced involved restructuring over 12 different store cards, credit cards, and loans which transformed the situation for the client, who was facing financial ruin, to clear all those debts in 3 years.

According to data from CNBC money, millennials aged 25-34 have the most debt, at an average of $42,000. Credit card balances make up the largest part, followed by student loans, and mortgages only a small part (3%). Naturally enough, this changes as we get older when mortgage debt becomes the most significant component followed by credit cards, car loans, then student debt. However, according to Kevin O'Leary, host of the ABC show Shark tank and personal finance author, age 45 is when "people should aim to have all their debt paid off". His logic is that for most people, they are halfway through their careers and working lives and so need to use the second half to accrue capital for their retirement. While I don't entirely agree with him (*I still have a mortgage because it costs me less than inflation*), he does make a sound point. Therefore, while it may be difficult for you to remember that you came to drain the swamp when you are fighting off hordes of alligators, it does pay to have a goal in mind. Right now, you are probably wondering just how you are going to stay afloat.

To illustrate the key points and provide motivation, this book contains some case studies to show that you can apply the same lessons to your situation. It also offers practical worked examples, where relevant, as this often makes a point better than a thousand words. Last but not least, I have included all the actionable points in the summary for each chapter.

Accept the need to act. Your debts are growing every day, start reading before your situation spirals beyond redemption, and decisions are taken out of your hands. This book contains all information that you will need to resolve your situation and sets out clearly and concisely how to tackle each problem.

CHAPTER ONE: MOVING THE DEBT MOUNTAIN

IN THIS DAY AND AGE, LIVING DEBT-FREE IS SOMETHING THAT IS nearly impossible to do. Most people have very limited resources and growing needs which are often very difficult to meet without taking on some kind of credit. It is common for people to take mortgages in order to purchase homes or acquire student loans to finance their higher education. Debt can therefore be a means to an end and a very practical way of financing some of our lives' biggest goals. However, in recent years, the issue of debt has taken on very negative connotations and most people tend to perceive debt as a bad thing - *which isn't always a fair assessment.* The truth of the matter is that debt is simply a tool whose benefits and or disadvantages depend entirely on how it is used. Understanding how debt works is therefore a very important aspect of financial literacy, which can help you to become more shrewd and disciplined with your money.

In this chapter, we are going to look at how debt works, when it becomes sustainable, and how to stabilize your debt to prevent it from ballooning out of control. We will also discuss the debts that you should prioritize and why to do so.

WHAT IS DEBT?

Debt essentially refers to anything that is owed by an individual *(or group)* to another. In modern parlance, debt is commonly used to refer to money or financial assets that one party owes to another. As we mentioned at the outset of this chapter, debt can be a very powerful financial tool that allows you to achieve certain goals or needs in life. This, however, depends to a large extent on the amount that you are credited with and how you handle it. Taking on a lot of debt or poorly managing the money that you borrow can lead to poor financial outcomes, which can easily destabilize your life. Understanding the difference between good and bad debt as well as how to handle debt the right way can help you ease your debt burden and improve your overall financial position.

What's the difference between good and bad debt?

In general, any kind of credit or loan that helps you to grow your income or increase your net worth can be considered as good debt. Some of the most common examples of good debt include:

- Student Loans

Taking on a loan to finance college or university education can be considered as a good debt for a number of reasons. First, acquiring a higher education automatically increases your earning potential. College graduates generally tend to earn more on average compared to employees who only have a high school diploma or less. Obviously, there are exceptions to this as well as a number of other factors that determine one's earnings in the job market. However, workers who have attained a college education are more likely to receive higher pay than those who haven't received a higher education even in entry-level positions. In addition to this, employees who are better educated have higher chances of finding new opportunities in the job market compared to those who have not gone through a university or college program. A student loan can therefore be considered as a good investment with the potential for high returns. However, in order to maximize the value of taking on this kind of debt, one should choose a degree program carefully. If there are very few career options or potential for income growth then a student loan can easily turn into bad debt. If a college uses misleading advertising to make false claims about job prospects that don't exist, then you may have a case against them and be able to overturn even your federal debts if these can be proven to be material.

- Mortgage/Homeownership

With property prices rising literally by the day, many people are increasingly turning to mortgage loans as a means to purchase homes and achieve a degree of financial independence. A mortgage is *arguably* the best debt one can take on. This is because it allows you to become a homeowner and cut down significantly on your spending *(you can finally say goodbye to monthly rent payments)*. This provides you with greater financial freedom since you can channel the surplus income towards paying off other debts and making investments, which will ultimately help you to grow your wealth. Residential and commercial properties also generally tend to appreciate in value over time, which means you can sell your property for a much higher price after a few years. Furthermore, mortgage loans tend to have a very low interest - *you can pay them comfortably over a given period of time as long as you are still earning some income.* The downside of mortgages occurs when you are unable to pay back the loan since your property may end up getting repossessed by your lender.

- Business Loans

Unless you have ready seed capital or are able to source funding from friends and relatives, you ostensibly need to take a loan when setting up a new business. During the first few months of setting up a business, expenses and operating costs tend to be higher than profits. Therefore, in order to keep your business afloat, you need to have a capital reserve, which will allow you to pay your suppliers, cover your operating costs, and pay salaries to employees. Getting a bank loan can help you to keep your business running until you are profitable enough to meet your outstanding expenses and even scale up. A business loan is therefore a good debt since it allows you to become financially independent *(your own boss)* and has a high potential of growing your wealth.

As you can see from all these examples, a good debt provides you with the opportunity to increase your earnings and grow your net worth. In contrast, bad debt is any kind of debt that you take on in order to purchase assets that don't generate any income but instead depreciate in value over time. As a rule of thumb, any kind of debt that leaves you worse off, in the long run, should be avoided since they can be catastrophic to your financial life and stability. Some of the most common examples of bad debts include:

- Car Loans

While owning a car provides you with greater freedom and mobility *(which can make your life and work easier)* taking a loan to purchase a vehicle is usually not a very wise decision. This is because you end up paying a lot of interest while the value of the car depreciates almost as soon as it leaves the showroom and continues to plummet with usage. If you must own a car, it is always best to purchase a used one and pay cash. You may not exactly end up with a luxury car that gets everyone talking, but you will ultimately save on a lot of money and avoid the stress that you would otherwise have to deal with when servicing the high-interest rates that are often charged on car loans. If you don't have cash but still need a vehicle, you can take a small low-interest loan to buy an inexpensive but reliable car and try to pay back the loan as quickly as possible. You will still have spent a huge amount of money on a depreciating asset but at least you won't have to pay high-interest rates, which can put a serious dent into your finances.

- Credit Cards

Credit cards are without a doubt the second-worst debt that one can take on (after pay day loans). This is because they tend to have the highest interest rates of any kind of consumer loans. In addition to this, the payment schedules are usually set up to favor the creditor. Most people who default on credit card payments often end up accruing very high interests, which they are stuck paying for months or even years.

- Clothes and Consumables

While there is nothing explicitly wrong with buying expensive clothes, phones, and other consumables, acquiring these products on credit is usually a bad idea in most cases. This is because these items do not grow your income in any way and typically lose value very quickly. Every cent that you spend paying back debt on these items is money that you would otherwise put to better use elsewhere. Which is why it is always advisable to purchase them in cash. Fortunately, there are a lot of options and alternatives which you can use to acquire these products without having to take on debts. Instead of taking credit to purchase expensive designer clothes, you are better off buying inexpensive but good quality clothes from a thrift shop.

TYPES OF DEBT- SECURED VS UNSECURED DEBT

There are two main types of debt, namely: secured and unsecured debt. Understanding the characteristics of these different types of debt is crucial because it enables you to know which debts to prioritize when it comes to payment.

Secured debt essentially refers to any kind of debt that has an asset attached to it as collateral. The most common assets that are normally used as collateral are houses *(for mortgage loans)* and cars *(for automobile loans)*. These assets provide lenders with leverage, which they can use to recoup their money and minimize the risk of loss. If an individual fails to clear their outstanding debt, then the lender has a right to claim their property. For instance, if you take a mortgage to buy a house and are unable to pay it back, the lender can legally repossess and sell the house to recoup their money. If the sale value is not enough to cover the entire debt, then they may continue to pursue you until they recover the deficit. An automobile loan is also another type of secured debt since the lender can repossess and resell the vehicle if the debtor fails to clear the debt as agreed.

In general, a person who takes up a loan to purchase an asset never fully owns it until they have cleared the outstanding debt. Once the full payment has been made to the lender, the transfer of ownership on the asset is completed.

Unlike secured debts, which are backed by collateral (*recoupable assets*), unsecured debts generally have no collateral rights attached to them and instead rely on the debtor's promise to pay back what they owe. Therefore, the lender cannot make any claim on the assets if the debtor defaults on payment. However, they can employ other avenues to coax the debtor to repay the debt. For instance, they can hire a debt collector to persuade the debtor to clear their debt. If this fails to work, they can file a lawsuit against the person who owes them and convince the court to garnish a percentage of the person's salary, which is then redirected towards debt repayment. Some of the most common examples of unsecured debts include credit card debts, student loans, and medical bills.

IS YOUR DEBT UNSUSTAINABLE?

As we have seen from the previous section, debt is not automatically a bad thing, provided it is used for income-generating ventures and is paid back as soon as possible to avoid an accumulation of interest. Gauging your debt level is therefore very important when it comes to figuring out which debts to prioritize. However, identifying a debt problem isn't always easy to do.

There are several signs that can help you to determine whether you have a personal debt crisis. These include:

- Making Minimum Payments

While low payments provide you with flexibility and enable you to meet other financial obligations while still servicing your debt, making minimum payments is likely to keep you stuck in a cycle of revolving debt payments. Meanwhile, your interest continues to rack up, which means you end up paying more.

- Very Large Minimum Monthly Payments

If you are making very large minimum monthly payments to service your debt, you are going to have a very difficult time meeting your living costs, and may even end up racking up more debt just to compensate for the deficit. In an ideal situation, your monthly debt payments should not exceed 20% of your income.

- Problems with Debt Collectors

When creditors and debt collectors start hounding you constantly or threatening to garnish your wages and repossess your assets, this is a tell-tale sign that your debt has become unsustainable. If you are still earning some income, you should start making payments towards your debt to lower it, and stop your creditors from making such threats.

- Over-Reliance on Advance Cash

If you regularly take cash advances to cover your living expenses, then you are likely stuck in a debt problem. Cash advances should ideally be used only in emergency situations and repaid promptly to avoid racking up interest.

- Being Denied Loans/Credit

In case you are trying to secure a loan from a bank or other lender but are constantly getting turned down, you need to take a step back and examine your debt situation. Chances are your credit rating is very poor due to non-payment or minimum payment, which makes lenders very wary about extending any more credit to you. On the off chance that you do get a lender who is willing to give you a loan, their terms are likely going to be very unfavorable.

- Not Growing Your Savings

Your budget should always include a savings plan of some kind, whether it is an emergency fund, retirement savings, or college fund for your kids. If you always end up with nothing to save after sorting out your expenses and paying bills then you probably have a serious debt crisis.

In order to manage your debt and maintain a good credit rating, it is important to know your debt-to-income ratio. A debt-to-income ratio (DTI) is essentially a metric that compares your overall debt to your income. Lending institutions typically use your DTI to determine whether you are able to make monthly payments and clear your debt within the agreed duration.

Having a good DTI, therefore, implies that you have a good balance between your outstanding debts and total income. On the other hand, a high DTI means that you have too much debt compared to your income. Generally, you have higher chances of securing a loan if your DTI percentage is low.

So, how does one determine their debt-to-income ratio?

Well, in order to calculate your DTI, you simply need to sum up all your monthly debt payments and divide them by your gross monthly income. Your gross income is essentially what you earn every month before taxes and other deductions are made.

To illustrate how DTI is calculated, let us assume that you pay $1500 every month for your mortgage, $500 on a car loan, and $500 for other monthly debt payments. Your total debt payment can be calculated by summing up all these payments.

$1500 + $500 + $500 = $2500

If your gross monthly income is $5000, then your DTI can be calculated as follows:

2500/5000 = 0.5 x 100 = 50%

This would be considered high because if taxes take around another 30% - 35% of your income this would leave you only $750 to $,1000 for the rest of your needs and wants.

In general, lenders are more likely to loan you money if your DTI is less than 36% with no more than 28% of that going to mortgage payments. However, your DTI ratio does not really affect your credit score directly since credit agencies are not privy to your earnings and are therefore unable to make this calculation.

Total Debt Repayments each month	Level of Risk
Less than 30% of you pre-tax monthly income	You are in good shape
Between 31% and 36% of pre-tax income	OK
Between 37% and 40% of pre tax income	Cut your spending and pay down debt
Over 40% of monthly pre-tax income	Take drastic steps to cut spending and pay off debt

Nevertheless, keeping your debt-to-credit ratio is still very important since it determines the ease with which you are able to secure loans from lenders. There are two ways in which you can cut down on your DTI ratio. One of the ways to do so is by increasing your income. You can achieve this in a number of ways such as requesting a pay rise from your employer, finding another job or side hustle to supplement what you are currently earning, completing another course, or program to improve your marketability and raise your salary. Alternatively, you can reduce your DTI by cutting down on your spending and minimize debts.

REASONS WHY YOU MAY BE SINKING IN DEBT

Controlling your debt is crucial if you want to take charge of your finances and achieve the goals that you have set for yourself. In order to do so, however, you need to get to the root of why you are in debt. Understanding why you have so much debt in the first place can help you to identify the mistakes that you have been making and how to solve them in order to be debt-free or have sustainable debt.

If you are wondering why you are sinking into so much debt, here are some of the top reasons why you may find yourself in that situation.

1. Living beyond Your Income

One of the most common reasons why you may be struggling with debt is because you are trying to maintain a lifestyle that is beyond your income. You may be spending too much money purchasing expensive and flashy items in a bid to keep up with others, which inevitably forces you to take on a lot of debt to furnish that lifestyle.

2. Overspending

Sometimes all it takes to get yourself trapped in a cycle of debt is failing to rein in your spending. You don't necessarily have to be buying luxury items, but spending too much on living costs can easily result in a blowup of debt.

3. Reduced Income

If your income suddenly reduces due to losing your job, for instance, this can put a dent in your budget and force you to take on debt in order to meet your living costs. This is why many financial experts usually advise people to diversify their sources of income.

4. Little or No Savings

One of the reasons why including savings in your budget is always recommended is because it provides you with a financial cushion in case of unexpected events. Ask, yourself this. Suppose you lost your job today, would you still be able to maintain your current lifestyle? If you have not been saving part of your income in an emergency fund, chances are you would have a hard time staying afloat unless you take on some kind of debt.

THE COST OF DEBT

Whenever you take credit, whether it is a mortgage, a payday loan, or a student loan, you are essentially using someone else's money today with the promise of paying it back in the future. Since the individual or institution that lends you the money does not have access to it until you pay it back, they have to charge interest on top of the loaned amount.

Interest is the cost that one is charged for using borrowed money. An alternative way of thinking about interest is that it is the profit that an individual or institution earns from lending money to another party. Interest is normally calculated as a percentage of a loan that is payable to a lender for the privilege of using their funds. Whenever you borrow money, you always have to pay back the total amount in addition to an interest, which is charged to compensate the lender for the risk of lending their money.

So, how much interest does one pay when they take out a loan?

Well, this depends on a number of factors such as the amount of loan, interest rate, and duration of repayment. In

CHAPTER ONE: MOVING THE DEBT MOUNTAIN

general longer-term loans and loans with high-interest rates tend to result in higher costs for the borrower. Credit card loans, payday loans, and to a lesser extent, car loans are typically charged much higher interest rates compared to mortgage loans. Taking any of these loans is therefore likely to be very costly in the long run.

To illustrate how costly debt can be, consider the following table:

	Mortgage	Vehicle loan	Credit Card	PayDay
Amount borrowed	$300,000	$30,000	$3,000	$300
Simple interest rate	4.7% annual	8.64% annual	25.6% annual	20% for 14 days
APR (excluding fees)	5.0%	9.0%	29%	521%
Term of Loan	30 years	3 years	1 Year	1 year
Interest to be paid	**$996,582**	**$8,467**	**$870**	**$1,563**
Total amount owed	$1,296,582	$38,467	$3,870	$1,863

Interest on all loans is assumed to have a monthly compounding when a debtor fails to pay interest on a given month. The only exception to this rule is payday loans, which are typically compounded fortnightly (*every two weeks*). The interest to be paid is the total amount of interest that one owes assuming you make no payments over the duration of the loan. This means that for the payday loan you borrow only $300 but you have to pay back an eye-watering $1,863 if you borrowed the money for 1 year (normally you are expected to pay it back within 14 days, which makes it seem reasonable, when in fact it is usurious).

The fees for non-payment of interest can be very high, especially for payday loans and credit card loans. In some cases, they can ever be more than twice the amount of annualized percentage rate (APR).

The annualized percentage rate is essentially simple interest expressed in a way that allows for comparing different compounding periods.

UNDERSTAND YOUR BUDGET

The number one reason why most people usually find themselves sinking in debt is simply that they spend more than they earn. In other words, they don't live within the confines of their budget. If you are struggling with debt, therefore, understanding your budget and optimizing it to suit your income and expenses is absolutely important. Let us now look at some of the steps you need to take in order to budget appropriately and cut down on your debt a lot faster.

- Track Your Spending

In order to determine whether your expenditure exceeds your income, you need to start keeping track of your monthly spending. Make a list of every penny that you spend on everything from food, clothing, entertainment, and utilities. You can either go the traditional way of writing down your spending with a notebook and pen or take advantage of the numerous budgeting apps that are available today. I provide a budgeting sheet as part of my free financial toolkit.

- Add up Your Total Expenditure and Income

Once you have determined your total monthly spending, the next thing you need to do is add that with your income. This will help you to easily tell if you are spending more than you are earning. Consequently, you will be able to identify the changes that you need to make in order to make your budget more practical.

- Create a Budget

If you have realized that your spending exceeds your

income, you need to make cuts to your spending until it is less than your income. Ideally, you should make a budget first and then look at the areas where you may need to cut down in order to reduce your spending. By creating a budget and sticking to it, you will eliminate the tendency to overspend and cut down on your borrowing habits - *which are keeping you stuck in debt.*

The table below compares the difference in what will happen to your wealth if you either spend $100 more than you earn (the debtor), or spend $100 less than you earn *(the investor).*

	Debtor	Investor
Cost or return	23%	9%
Cashflow	$ -100	$ 100
Year 1	$ -1,338	$ 1,254
Year 2	$ -2,984	$ 2,621
Year 3	$ -5,008	$ 4,111
Year 4	$ -7,498	$ 5,735
Year 5	$ -10,560	$ 7,505

In the debtor column, you have a negative cash flow *(earning – expenditure)* per month of $100, after 1 year you will owe $1,388 of debt, finishing owing $10,560 after 5 years based on the 23% APR. On the other side, $100 positive cash flow based on a 9% return on investment in the stock market *(which is conservative the returns have been in excess of 11% over a thirty-year period)* then you finish with an investment of $7,505 after 5 years.

- Establish an Emergency Fund

If you are earning a monthly income, it is absolutely important that you put a percentage of that into an emergency fund. As a matter of fact, many financial experts usually recommend creating an emergency fund before saving money for other goals such as retirement or vacations. Ideally, you should put at least 10% of your income in an emergency fund until you have enough funds to meet your living expenses for at least 3 months. Having an emergency fund provides you with a measure of financial security in the event of unforeseen occurrences such as job loss, car breakdown, or medical emergencies. Without an emergency fund to cater for these unexpected expenses, you may end up having to take on credit, which can make your debt situation even worse.

Here are some of the key points to take away from this chapter:

- Debt can be a good thing or a bad thing depending on how it is utilized and repaid
- Any debt that helps you increase your income or improve your financial situation can be considered as good debt. Examples include mortgage loans, student loans, and investment loans
- Any kind of debt that is used to purchase consumer items or depreciating assets is a bad debt, which should be avoided. Examples of this include, car loans, and credit card loans
- Creating and maintaining a workable budget will help you keep your spending in check and avoid borrowing too much.
- Maintaining a low debt-to-income ratio is very important since it proves your debt is sustainable and makes lenders more confident about your ability to pay back loans.

CHAPTER TWO: WHEN CREDITORS ATTACK

IN THIS CHAPTER WE ARE GOING TO LOOK AT THE PROCESS YOU will experience when creditors turn their debt collection tactics onto you. A subsequent chapter will then talk you through some of the strategies you can employ to fight back. So, you have realized that you are neck-deep in debt, are struggling with minimum payments and suddenly your creditors are hounding you from every side and making demands. This is very common, about 15% of Americans, or nearly 50 million people said that they had been sued by debt collectors at some point, a staggering number.

You can expect the debt collection process to begin once you are 30 days overdue if you make no payment. It will probably start with a letter or email, and the calls will start shortly thereafter. Initially, the calls are likely to be with a customer service team rather than specialist collections teams. Each organization varies, but the debt will not normally be transferred to the collections teams until it is between 60 and 90 days overdue. At this point, if you haven't spoken to them, then you will probably get other emails or letters too.

Some banks or lenders will continue to manage the collections and recovery process in-house, until such point as they sell the debt. Other lenders will outsource this to an agency at an early stage. More banks are dealing with this in-house for longer, especially secured creditors.

All debt collections calls will have similar characteristics. Those from agencies rather than the original lender are likely to be more aggressive and try to use scare tactics to persuade you to pay. We have a section below on how to manage these calls and talk through what to do and what NOT to do. The process is similar regardless of who is making the calls

From 30 days overdue, your lender will begin to report your debt as overdue to the credit bureaux and this will begin to impact your credit rating. More discussion of this in the next chapter. For unsecured debts *(e.g. credit cards, store cards, medical, private student loans)*, at some point in the process - if the lender has exhausted their own remediation - they may sell the debt on to a debt collection agency (your account is then in collections). This may also happen for some secured lending too, but they may manage foreclosure proceeding internally, only selling the debt if these fail.

At some point (possibly around 90 days plus overdue) lenders may instigate legal proceedings. You may be served writs to attend a court hearing, as a result of which the lender may obtain a judgment against you to recover the debt. That essentially is the process, after that point, it will be dependent very much on the type of debt.

BASIC TERMINOLOGY

There are a few terms that we will commonly use throughout the book, but may not be widely understood. There is a more comprehensive glossary at the back of the book but that is more tricky to use on e-readers, so I wanted to include selected terminology here:

- Creditor: This is the bank/lending institution (or a personal acquaintance in bankruptcy proceedings) that a debt is owed to.
- Original Creditor (OC): The creditor to whom the original debt is owed to. This is very important when dealing with debt collection agencies (DCA).
- Debtor: This is the person (or business) that owes a debt to a creditor.
- Credit Reporting Agency: These are the 3 major reporting agencies or credit bureaux: TransUnion (TU), Equifax (EQ), and Experian (EXP) which list, and then report the history of your credit

DELINQUENT & DEFAULT

Delinquency occurs when a borrower fails to make a payment on their loan. Whereas, default happens when a person fails to repay their loan as stated in the contract. Creditors usually allow loans to remain delinquent, before considering them in default. However, this depends on the type of loan and the creditor involved. Many consider mortgages to be delinquent once they are 90 days *(3 months)* behind in payment.

Once you hit 90 days overdue with a payment, your loan will be reported to the main CRA as officially delinquent.

Just one collection account (usually accounts that are officially delinquent are moved to collections) can cause a credit score to drop 50 to 100 points, but this won't last forever. Unless there are new negative events, your score will steadily improve over time. Collections may remain on your credit report for seven years from the date of the original delinquency. This statute of limitations holds true for both paid and unpaid accounts (with few exceptions). Sometimes you can negotiate with a CA to remove the entry in a 'Pay for Delete, however, they don't have to agree to this, and in some cases, they are not able to do so, as it is the prerogative of the OC.

Once you are 270 days overdue, it will be considered to be in default, and at that point, many lenders will charge it off. That is to say, it will be written up as bad debt in their financial accounts. Again, this is a rule of thumb and can't be considered hard and fast for all loans and situations. Note that the U.S. federal government allows student debt to be delinquent for 270 days before declaring it to be in default.

Very often, this will be the point the original lender will sell the unsecured debt to a debt collections agency. Federal student debt is not treated in the same way, although a collections agency may be retained. Being in default will also be reported to the CRAs.

HOW DO DEBT COLLECTION AGENCIES WORK?

Debt collection agencies (DCAs) are businesses that are tasked to collect debts on behalf of creditors or lenders. In other words, debt collection agencies act as middlemen between debtors and lenders. There are two main types of DCA, namely hired collection agencies and agencies that buy debt from the original creditor.

- Hired Debt Collection Agencies

These are businesses that are tasked to collect debts that are overdue by at least 60 days on behalf of a creditor or lender. Hired debt collectors usually earn a percentage of the collected money, which varies between 25-50%. These agencies usually act as middlemen who collect various types of debts, including car loans, medical bills, student loans, and even utility bills. Hired debt collection agencies only get paid when they collect your debts and increase their earnings by collecting more debt.

- Debt-Buying Agencies

When an original creditor has decided that pursuing debtors is not something they are prepared to do, they may opt to cut their losses by selling the debt to a debt-buying agency. In most cases, creditors will bundle together several different debts with similar features and sell them to the buying agency as a package. Debt-buying agencies usually purchase these packages through bidding. On average, debt-buying agencies pay about 4 cents per every $1 of debt that they buy from a creditor. This, however, can vary depending on the duration that the debt has been unpaid. Older debts are usually priced much lower than recent ones since they are riskier and less likely to be collectible.

HOW DO DEBT COLLECTORS OPERATE?

Debt collectors usually reach out to delinquent debtors via phone calls and letters to try and convince them to pay their outstanding debt. In cases where debt collectors are unable to reach debtors through the information provided by creditors, they may resort to hiring private investigators to aid their search. In addition to communicating with debtors, collectors also conduct investigations on debtor assets, which can be used as leverage in case the borrowers are unable to pay back what they owe. Sometimes, debt collectors may report defaulting debtors to credit bureaus as a way of encouraging them to make payment. Poor credit ratings can seriously affect a borrower's credit score and make it difficult for them to secure loans in the future.

It is important to realize that debt collection is a legally recognized business. So, if you are behind on your debt payments and collectors start calling you, resist the urge to lash out at them, ultimately they are just people going about their job.

In the next chapter, we will discuss how to handle these calls when managing our debts.

HELP! I AM BEING TAKEN TO COURT!

First up, don't worry, you are not going to jail. Debtors' jails are something from a bygone age. Getting served just means that you have been given notice of a lawsuit, You are served if you are handed a copy of the summons and complaint or someone of suitable age is handed a copy, at your address. If the lawsuit is against you, you are the defendant. If the lawsuit names you as a defendant, you must respond, even if you think the debt is not yours! The person or party initiating the complaint is the plaintiff.

The summons and complaint (the process) are a statement of the claims against you and a notice of the lawsuit. The lawsuit now starts even if it is not filed with the court. This is important because it means there may not be a court filing number. Therefore if you contact the court, they may tell you it has no record of the case. But that does not mean the process has not started as the creditor has up to a year from the date of service to file with the court.

The language used by most collection agencies is designed to create fear - for them, that is part of the process because they want you to settle. Once you are served with a lawsuit, you may be tempted to ignore it completely. And if you fail to answer the complaint, the creditor can get a default judgment after the 20-day response period, which means you have lost the case before it begins. You will not have a court date and you will not have an opportunity to talk to a judge if you decide not to respond.

JUDGMENT

A court will enter a judgment against you in case the creditor wins their case or if you fail to show up in court. You will receive the notice of judgment entry via mail. The creditor may use the judgment to collect cash. Common methods used include garnishment *(wages and bank accounts)*, property attachments *(this can be any asset you own)*, and property liens *(liens apply to the building and land)*.

State laws control the amount of money and types of property a creditor with a judgment can collect. These laws vary state by state, so you need to check the laws that apply to you.

The initial debt amount may now include attorney fees, filing fees, interest, etc - *anything related to the case.*

Receiving a judgment resets the Date of First Delinquency (DOFD) automatically to a date the judgment was made, and it is the only solution for changing the DOFD. The reporting time on debt *(relating to the statute of limitations)* is now seven years from the time the judgment was made.

The judgment stays active for ten years (or 20 years in some states). Therefore, a collection agency has ten years to collect judgment owed. In case they fail, a judgment to reset for an additional 10 years may be given. This means the collection agency can reset the clock indefinitely until the debt is cleared

WAGE GARNISHMENTS AND FROZEN BANK ACCOUNTS

One of the strategies that lenders often apply to recover their money from a debtor is wage garnishment. Once a creditor has obtained a judgment, they can then get a court order to enforce it. This typically happens through a court that directs that your employer withholds a certain percentage of your paycheck and sends it to the person who is owed until all the debt is cleared. Some of the most common sources of wage garnishment include student loans, consumer debts, and child support. In all of these instances, your wages will be garnished until the debt is fully settled. However, just because a court orders your paycheck to be garnished it doesn't mean that you have no reprieve whatsoever. As a matter of fact, the law puts caps on the amount that can be garnished from your wages in order to ensure that you still keep part of your earnings for your own personal use.

There are two types of garnishment which a court can order:

1. Wage Garnishment

This gives your employer the authority to slash off part of your paycheck and hand over the money to your creditors

Wage garnishment generally happens when a creditor sues an individual who is indebted to them for non-payment and wins. However, there are several instances when a creditor can enforce a garnishment without a court order, for instance, non-payment of child support or failure to pay federal student loans.

So, how much of your wage can be garnished by court order? Well, this generally varies depending on the state that you live in. Some states like California have a cap of 25% when it comes to wage garnishment. For ordinary garnishments (those not for support, bankruptcy, or any state or federal tax), the weekly amount may not exceed the lesser of two figures: 25% of the employee's disposable earnings, or the amount by which an employee's disposable earnings are greater than 30 times the federal minimum wage (currently $7.25 an hour or $217.50). So if your disposable weekly income is less than this ($217.50) you cannot have your wages garnished, but every single dollar earned above that can be seized until the point you earn more than $290, when it reverts to 25%. Wage garnishments for child support payments usually tend to be very high, typically capping at around 60%. Student loans, on the other hand, have much lower garnishment caps - normally peaking at 15%.

In some states, the law exempts debtors from wage garnishment if they are the head of a household or breadwinner for a family. While filing for bankruptcy can provide some immediate protection against wage and non-wage garnishment, it does not protect the debtor from garnishment once a court has ordered a repayment plan for all the debts owed. In instances where the money is owed for federal taxes, a court order is not required before a garnishment can be enforced. Usually, the Internal Revenue Service (IRS) will send a Notice of Demand for Payment to the debtor. This is followed by a Final Notice which provides the debtor with a 30 day period to clear what is owed. If the payment is not completed by the debtor, the IRS will contact the debtor's employer and begin the wage garnishment.

2. Freezing your bank account - Non-wage Garnishment

Creditors and federal agencies can seize your bank account and use the money contained therein to clear your debts, they do not always require a court judgment against you to do so.

For account holders who have their loan accounts at the same institution as their bank account, the lender can access your account(s) to pay the defaulted loans without filing a lawsuit or judgment. When you sign for the loan, you give the bank full access to your account in the event of default. Default is normally 270 days overdue, but actual timing would be defined in your loan contract and could be significantly less.

If they have a court judgment, other creditors can get the bank to freeze your account to repay what you owe. The court order and judgment is sent to the bank and kept on file. You'll get notified that a creditor has levied your bank account. The notice will describe the bank account and will explain how you can claim any exemptions that will allow you to keep some or all of your money.

If you owe taxes to the government, the IRS can freeze your bank account and it won't be lifted until they are paid in full.

A frozen account means you won't have access to any of your money until the situation is resolved. This means you can't take out any money and scheduled payments won't go through. Because these payments will probably bounce, you'll incur a non-sufficient funds (NSF) charge. If you have money in your account, this will deplete your balance. If not, you'll dip into a negative balance, putting you into an overdraft. In this case, you'll have to pay additional fees and interest to cover the shortfall.

There are some exemptions that allow you to keep some or all of your money even if a creditor has a judgment against you. The amount you may keep from seizure depends on the total amount in your account, its source, and specific laws in your state.

Some federal benefits can't be seized like Social Security, Supplemental Security Income (SSI), or veterans' benefits.

Under this law, the bank must protect two months' worth of federal benefits if the funds were directly deposited into the account. However, if the garnishment relates to the recovery of child support, spousal support, federal student loans, or federal taxes, the bank can freeze the funds, even if they come from Social Security. SSI is protected from garnishment even if the debt is a government, child support, or spousal support debt.

SEIZURE OF PROPERTY

When a creditor moves to court, they have the right to stake a claim on your property in a bid to recoup their money. However, just because a court makes a ruling that your property can be seized doesn't automatically mean your property will be handed over to your creditor. The creditor is obliged to discharge or satisfy the debt that is owed to them. If you are in deep debt and at risk of getting your assets seized, therefore, you need to know which assets are seizable and what strategies you can employ to minimize the likelihood of asset forfeiture.

Once a judgment has been made by a court of law, the onus lies with the creditor to decide how to proceed with the forfeiture. They will need to establish which assets are seizable. This is normally accomplished through a judgment debtor's examination, which helps to unearth the assets or properties that can be forfeited by the creditor. In addition to this, the creditor should have a good understanding of the properties that are exempted from seizure.

Each state provides certain exemptions on a debtor's assets that can be claimed by a creditor. If all of the debtor's remaining assets fall under certain limits, then the judgment may be rendered as hollow or unenforceable. There are also asset protection trusts which allow you to transfer your assets to an independent trustee who shields them from creditors. Alternatively, you can transfer your assets to a spouse's name to put them out of the reach of creditors who may be trying to claim them. As a rule of thumb, you should always keep your business assets separate from personal assets in order to avoid repossession by creditors.

Debtor Assets and Properties that are Seizable

When most people think of seizable property, the first thing that usually comes to mind is real estate. However, in a forfeiture claim, the assets that can be seized by a creditor include not only the house that you live in but also assets that you own such as cars, boats, and even hard cash. In some instances, this can also extend to your salary, financial assets such as stocks and bonds, your deposit accounts, and even IRA accounts. If you file for bankruptcy, for example, a creditor can seek a court order to have your stocks garnished if they are held in a non-retirement account. Most people tend to assume that since they don't own the house that they live in or any tangible assets like cars or money in the bank, then a creditor can't seize anything from them. This, however, is a very fatalistic assumption since a creditor who is determined to recoup what they are owed can stake a claim on virtually anything that you own.

Nevertheless, there are certain exemptions that can protect you from losing some of your assets in the event that a court gives a forfeiture judgment. This, of course, varies from state to state. In most jurisdictions, a creditor is allowed to make a claim on your home, which means you can lose your house if you are unable to pay back secured debts. In the case of unsecured debts such as credit card debts and payday loans, however, your creditor cannot make any claim on your assets. If you live in a rented property or a house that is owned by someone else, judgment creditors are also not allowed to claim it since you don't have the right to give it away or sell it.

If you give away a property that you own in order to protect it from forfeiture, your creditor may be able to sue you for attempted fraud. This may result in your property being repossessed and given to your creditor. Furthermore, you can be fined or prosecuted in a court of law for deliberately attempting to defraud your creditor. We will discuss this avenue later in the book among the more aggressive debt management strategies

A creditor who has a judgment against you can also go after property that you are entitled to but haven't possessed yet, especially once your right to the property has been firmly established. This may include salaries and commissions that you earned prior to or after the judgment has been made, severance pays, refunds, insurance payouts, royalties, and inheritance. One of the ways in which you can protect yourself from this process is to make sure that all your assets are owned by your partner, spouse, or other parties.

A creditor doesn't always have to forfeit your property after a judgment has been made. Sometimes, they may opt to attach a judgment lien on a property that you own, usually real estate (building and land). A lien is essentially a notice which stipulates that you owe a certain debt. This is normally filed with the register of deeds in the jurisdiction where the property is located. A judgment lien gives a creditor the right to collect their debt from the money that is made from the sale of the property. In most states, judgment liens usually have a validity period of 5 years and creditors are allowed to renew them until the judgment expires. However, there are a number of exceptional circumstances under which a creditor cannot seek a judgment lien. These include bankruptcy and foreclosure. Furthermore, a creditor cannot attach a lien on your property if there is one already in place.

FORECLOSURES

A foreclosure is a process through which a mortgage investor or lender repossesses a house when an individual fails to make their mortgage payments. Foreclosures are often triggered by a change in an individual's financial position, which makes them unable to meet their mortgage obligations. Some of the most common causes of foreclosures include medical problems that make one unable to work, too much debt, and sudden unemployment.

HOW FORECLOSURES WORK

There are two types of foreclosures; judicial and non-judicial foreclosures. In a judicial foreclosure, a lender typically brings a legal action against a debtor to court. This usually takes longer since each step of the process takes a period of between 30 to 90 days. On the other hand, non-judicial foreclosures take less time and do not require court action. They are instead based on the "power of sale" close that a lender has signed with their borrower.

Regardless of the type of foreclosure, your lender will serve you with a written notice to clear your outstanding debt followed by a "Notice of Default" (if you fail to make the payment) and a "Notice of Sale". If you feel that the foreclosure is unfair or you need more time to clear the payment, you can contest a foreclosure in a court. If you are facing a judicial foreclosure, a court will typically serve you with summons so you can make your case and challenge the foreclosure. However, if you are dealing with a non-judicial foreclosure, you will need to take legal action against your lender to stop the process of foreclosure.

In some states, the law requires a lender to provide their debtor with the option of reinstating the loan in order to halt the process. This allows you to continue living on the property after the Notice of Sale until the 'sale date' provided you settle the payments that you have defaulted on. You can also be granted the opportunity to clear the entire loan, although this is only possible if you can secure a substantial amount of money or refinance the home.

If you are unable to stop the foreclosure, the property will be put on auction by a court so that interested individuals can bid for its purchase. However, if no buyer is found, ownership of the house will be automatically transferred to the lender. If you have not made plans to protect the house and are still living in it, you face eviction and should start looking for alternative accommodation.

In most states, the law offers you a certain period within which you can reclaim your house after a foreclosure. This redemption period is usually indicated in the 'Notice of Sale'. However, you will have to be willing to clear the loan payment in addition to the costs incurred by the lender during the process of foreclosure before you can reclaim your home.

CONSEQUENCES OF FORECLOSURE

Going through a foreclosure can pose serious challenges to you as a debtor. The most obvious outcome of a foreclosure is that you may end up losing your house and getting evicted. This means you will be forced to look for accommodation elsewhere *(renting a house)*, which will inevitably take a toll on your personal and financial life.

Foreclosures are also generally very expensive processes that can make you lose a lot of money. When you default on your loan payments, your lender may charge you exorbitant late fees. In addition to this, you might end up incurring a lot of legal fees as you try to fight the foreclosure. Any extra fees that a lender imposes on you ultimately increase the amount that you owe them, and you may find yourself still indebted to them even after your house has been foreclosed and sold if the proceeds of the sale are not enough to cover all your debt.

Similarly, a foreclosure can severely impact your credit score. Once a lender initiates a foreclosure, your credit score will reflect this a month or two after the proceedings have begun and will remain that way for up to 7 years. This can seriously hamper your ability to secure another mortgage loan, even though you may still be eligible for some government loans. In some cases, a foreclosure can also hurt your chances of securing employment.

Filing a bankruptcy claim may temporarily stop a foreclosure from proceeding. However, the process is often very complex and may vary from state to state. It is therefore important to seek advice from a qualified attorney on the best course of action.

In conclusion, here are some of the key takeaways to remember from this chapter:

- Always respond to lawsuits and summonses because if you don't they likely get a default judgment against you.
- Lenders can resort to wage garnishments and seizing money from your bank account as a means of recovering the money that you owe them
- Failing to clear your mortgage loans can put you at risk of losing your house and getting evicted
- There are several steps that you can take to stop

foreclosures and garnishments including negotiating with your creditors, filing a bankruptcy claim, and debt consolidation/refinancing.
- In the next chapter, we will look at a range of strategies that you can deploy to frustrate or halt debt collection activity.

CHAPTER THREE: DEBT DESTRUCTION STRATEGIES

In the last chapter, we looked at the processes which your creditors will use to pursue you and recover their debts. By the time we got to judgment and foreclosures, it was all quite intimidating. However there are a number of things that you can do to resist or even thwart these processes, but to use them effectively, you must understand your rights and some of the side effects that they will generate. I am going to start by outlining a range of strategies from the most compliant to the most extreme. At this end of the spectrum, you will need patience, perseverance, and a steady nerve. Some of these strategies overlap or even run on from one another. You can also employ different strategies for each debt if you wish. For example, you might draw the line at using some of them for your mortgage, as you don't want to risk losing your house.

We are going to examine the following strategies, with a chapter dedicated to most approaches

- Pay the debts using debt snowball or debt avalanche methods

- Consolidate the debts to get lower payments using a debt consolidation loan
- Use a debt management plan to pay off loans over 3 to 5 years
- Negotiate and settle (or reduce the cost of) the debt
- Repudiate the debt
- Declare bankruptcy

Before we look at each of these, you need to understand some of the rights that the law gives you with respect to dealing with creditors and debt collections agencies and how you might deploy them, as this will benefit you regardless of which strategies you deploy.

FDCPA - KNOW YOUR RIGHTS

The Fair Debt Collection Practices Act (FDCPA) is a statute that was established in 1978 to mitigate unfair debt collection practices. Essentially it imposes a limit on the length of time that debts can be collected, known as the statute of limitations (SOL), this is explained below. Under this law, if a debt collector first contacts you about a debt, you should be notified of the right to dispute the debt and require 'verification' or 'validation'. The FDCPA does not apply to companies collecting their own debts. This act sets out legal parameters about who can be contacted, what they can say, when they can call, and how they can collect the debt, and it is worth understanding what rights are protecting you.

The FDCPA requires a debt collector to:

- Notify you of your right to dispute the debt within 30 days in addition to giving you the *'mini-*

Miranda' warning that anything you say may be
used towards the collection of the debt
- Verify the debt if you ask for the same within 30 days.

It is your prerogative as the debtor to dispute the debt within thirty days of receiving a notice of your rights. You should as a matter of course dispute the debt (to access my material for this go to www.PersonalFinanceWizard.com) and request verification then the debt collector can't proceed with collection until the debt is verified. Even if you feel that you owe something this is an opportunity to check and validate the amount.

It is worth noting that the purpose of this statute is not to establish a separate lawsuit (*against a creditor or debt collector*) but to protect consumers from unfair harassment resulting from mistaken identities and typo errors. When you dispute the debt, the debt collector is required to take action to connect you to it. If they cannot do this they cannot collect the debt.

DEBT VERIFICATION

Once you request a debt verification, the Collection Agency must stop the collection process. In case they continue, you may proceed to file a case. Interestingly, you can dispute a portion or the entire debt.

Once the collection notice is issued, the debtor only has thirty days to respond. If you don't respond to this notice, the debt is automatically assumed to be verified. In case the notice to verify your debt is given within thirty days of the first collection attempt, the Agency should stop the collection process until the required data that verifies your debt is provided

The first *(and most crucial)* step a CA should take when collecting a debt is to verify that you owe the said debt(s). Unfortunately, the CA is only required to provide:

- Name of creditor
- The amount of debt owed.

You should always request the CA to verify the debt *(in writing)*, as well as the address of the original creditor.

STATUTE OF LIMITATIONS FOR COLLECTING DEBTS

The Statute of limitations (SOL) is the amount of time allowed by a state (they are all different) in which legal proceedings may be brought against a debtor to collect on a debt. After that time expires, the debt is still owed but the collection cannot be enforced through the courts. The time is set from the date of first delinquency (DOFD) this is the date when payment was first missed.

Only a court judgment can reset the DOFD as we explained in chapter 2. This then gives the creditor or CA up to 10 years to collect.

Not only does the SOL vary by state, but also depends on the type of debt. For credit cards, and credit lines *(including in-store credit)* it can be as little as 3 years in many states, but 6 years is also common. Note that Rhode Island is an outlier at 10 years and in California, it is 4 years.

I have provided a link to a complete list, but please ensure that is up to date before relying on it: SOL by State and type of debt

If a creditor sues you after the collection period has expired, you can launch legal action against them. The chances of winning the case are very high, since you are only required to prove the debt is old. However, once you show your resolve and that you know your facts, they are likely to drop the case as you would have a case to counter sue for illegally attempting to collect a time-barred debt. Don't ignore it, however, take the necessary actions within five business days once you receive the summons. You may file a countersuit to prove that the SOL period on your debt has expired.

WHAT CAN RESET THE CLOCK ON SOL

It is possible for you to reset the clock on old debt and for them to become enforceable again. There is nothing to stop a CA from calling you about an old debt that has expired in terms of the SOL, remember that you still owe the money but it is not enforceable. In order to make sure that you don't accidentally restart the SOL clock, you need to be aware of the following:

- Acknowledging the debt in front of a creditor or a collector. Even verbal acknowledgment can restart the clock on an old debt.
- Making payments or partial payment on an old debt. Even making an agreement for paying can start the debt clock again.
- Accepting a settlement offer to pay off the old debt that has been expired.

Don't talk to CA about old debts. If they continue to harass you, then ask for a debt validation letter without acknowledging the debt. This does not restart the clock. You can then demand they stop contacting you.

THE FCRA AND YOUR CREDIT SCORE - KNOW YOUR RIGHTS

The Fair Reporting Credit Act (FRCA) is another statute that you can use to fight off debt collectors. It is a federal law created to enforce fairness, accuracy, and privacy of your information held in files of the credit reporting agencies (CRAs). This law grants you the right to dispute an item on your credit report, and also sets the time limit after which items must be removed. Typically the way it works is that you look at your credit report for anything that may be negative or inaccurate. In case you find anything that does not seem to add up, you can raise a dispute about it.

In order to exercise your credit dispute right properly, you need to get your credit report and dispute it with the CRA first before doing the same with any debt collector. This enables you to protect all your rights and avoid getting rolled over by your debt collectors. In case a debt collector fails to verify under the FDCPA, you can use this as the basis of your dispute with credit reference agencies using the terms of the FCRA.

You are entitled to request and receive all the information about you kept by a CRA. Sometimes, your request may require a fee, other times the disclosure is free of charge. According to the Federal Trade Commission (FTC), under the FCRA, you are entitled to a free file disclosure if:

- A person has taken adverse action against you because of information in your credit report
- You are the victim of identity theft and place a fraud alert in your file
- Your file has inaccurate data due to fraud
- You are on public assistance
- You don't have a job but expect to get/apply for a job within sixty days

- You are also entitled to one disclosure per year from each credit reporting agency

The information held and used by CRA is not the same as your credit score. You have the right to request your credit score, but you will have to pay for it.

If you follow the proper procedures to identify and report inaccurate or incomplete information, the CRA is legally bound to investigate your dispute. All inaccurate, incomplete, or unverifiable information must be corrected or removed within 30 days. *Correct information* does not have to be removed.

It is (usually) the case that negative information about you that is over 7 years old (and 10 years in the case of bankruptcy) can no longer be reported. For credit files, the 7 years are timed from the DOFD + up to 180 days.

The 7-year rule does not apply to all debts. There are four exceptions:

- Tax liens: 10 years if unpaid, or 7 years from payment date
- Bankruptcy: 10 years from the date of filing (15 U.S.C. §1681c)
- Federal student loans: As long as they are delinquent
- Judgments: Seven years/the debtor's state SOL on judgments - whichever is longer

WHO CAN SEE YOUR CREDIT FILE

A CRA may open your file to anyone that has a valid need to know, such as a business where you applied for credit, an insurance company you want to insure you, or a landlord.

However, employers (future or present) require your consent. My advice on this would be that bad credit episodes shouldn't hamper your employment unless it involves handling money, such as in a bank or as in a book-keeping role. The best way of dealing with this would be to tell a prospective employer upfront when they request your permission and explain the reason or history for the bad credit. It is after all very common.

PAYING OFF YOUR DEBTS IN A STRUCTURED APPROACH

I have included this section in the book for completeness, although it is not the primary approach I foresee for most readers. However, as I have already stated there are some debts where you may want to adopt this type of approach. This is also the reason for addressing it immediately in this chapter. The benefit of using one of these approaches is that it will maintain your credit score as far as possible.

Having multiple debts can lead to a sense of panic and leave you not knowing which way to turn. These methods provide a mechanism to prioritize and choose between debts and creditors. Unless you opt for debt consolidation and secure a loan to pay all your outstanding debts, chances are you will have to make a compromise in one way or another. There are two main strategies you can employ when choosing which debts to prioritize and pay first. Let us now go through each of them so that you can decide which method works best for you.

- Prioritizing Your Debt by Interest Rate (Debt Avalanche)

In this method (also known as *the avalanche method*), you

essentially prioritize your debt according to the interest rates charged from highest to lowest. By paying your debts with the highest interest rates first, you can save up more money over the course of your debt repayment journey since the interest that accrues in your accounts will decrease. This method allows you to accelerate your debt repayment much faster. Once you take out all the debts with high APR, your debt burden decreases significantly, and you are able to clear your low-interest debts more comfortably.

How to Use the Debt Avalanche Strategy

- List your debts on a worksheet in order from highest to lowest interest *(the debts with the highest APR should be at the top of the list and vice versa)*
- Review your budget to see which expenses you can cut down on and minimize your expenses as much as possible
- Make an entry of the total cash flow that you have for repaying your debts
- Subtract all minimum payment requirements from the total cash flow
- Add the remaining cash to the minimum payment on your first debt *(the one with the highest APR)* on the list. This will be your new avalanche payment
- Once the first debt is cleared, add the avalanche payment for that debt to the minimum payment of the second debt on your list
- Make avalanche payment on the second debt until that is cleared
- Repeat this process for each debt, always rolling the avalanche payment into the next debt on the list until all your debts are paid in full
- Prioritizing Your Debt According to Balance (Debt Snowball)

While the avalanche method is very cost-efficient, saving money is hardly the only consideration that you need to look for when coming up with a debt repayment strategy. If you are constantly stuck in a cycle of debt repayment, you may find it very difficult to save any money, which can take a toll on your motivation. You don't want to spend the rest of your life making minimum payments towards your debts.

The *debt snowball* method is a debt repayment strategy where you pay off the debts with lower balances first. This not only helps you build momentum a lot faster but also avails extra cash flow which you can then redirect to payment of larger debts. You are more likely to stick to your debt repayment strategy if you are achieving milestones in your journey.

How to use the Debt Snowball Method

- List all your debts on a worksheet in order of balance, from the lowest to the highest *(the debt with the lowest balance should be at the top of the list and vice versa)*
- Review your budget to cut down on your expenses and avail cash flow to be used for debt payment
- Write down the total cash flow that is available to you for debt repayment
- Subtract all your minimum payment requirements from the total cash flow
- Add this figure to the minimum payment on the first debt to come up with your new snowball payment.
- Make all minimum payments as scheduled, with the larger snowball payment on the first debt on your list
- Once the first debt is cleared, add the snowball

payment for that debt to the minimum payment of the second debt on your list
- Make the snowball payment on the second debt until it is paid in full
- Repeat this process for each debt, always adding the snowball payment into the minimum payment of the next debt until all your debts are paid in full.

MANAGING DEBT COLLECTION CALLS

Debt collection phone calls can be very overwhelming and intimidating, especially if you are caught off guard and don't have any solid plan in mind. Aggressive debt collectors can easily manipulate you into agreeing to a payment that you simply can't afford. You may even find yourself getting into a heated argument with a debt collector who demands payment immediately without bothering to listen to your situation. It is important to understand the right way to deal with debt collector calls in order to avoid situations that may exacerbate the predicament that you are faced with. Let us now look at some of the dos and don'ts that you should keep in mind when dealing with calls from debt collectors.

THINGS TO DO

1. Decide whether You really want to speak with the Collection Agent

In case you receive a call from a debt collector, you should consider hanging up first without speaking to them so that you can prepare yourself. Make sure the debt is really yours and fully understand your rights. This will help you to avoid mentioning things that can be used as leverage against you.

If a debt collector does get through to you and take you by surprise, you can hang up politely by giving a quick excuse, for example:

- I can't talk now because I am at work, and my employer doesn't allow personal calls.
- I can't talk now because I have people around.
- I can't talk now because I have an appointment and have to leave.

At some point in the process, usually around 30 days, it is probably worth answering a call, or calling your creditor and simply explain at that stage why you can't pay. This will help delay the onset of any legal process. You must stick with this story/argument thereafter to be consistent, so ensure it is properly thought through.

2. Keep a Call Log for Debt Collectors

A collection call log is a written record that allows you to keep track of your communication with debt collectors. Some of the details that you should include in your call log include the date and time of the call, the agent that you speak to, and what they say during the call. Your collector call log doesn't even have to be very complicated. Preferably you can use a notepad and pen. If you record the call, then ensure that you follow the relevant consent laws for your state. If it is a one-party consent, then simply state that you *(giving your name)* are recording the call. Do not elaborate further, do not ask for permission, do not apologize.

iii) Request the Collector to Cease Contact with You

If you feel uncomfortable about debt collectors hounding

you all the time and would like them to stop calling you, make your wishes clear in writing. You are within your rights to write to your creditors/debt collection agencies and ask them to desist from contacting you at work, due to your employer's policies.

You should realize that once you request debt collectors to stop making all contact with you, they will only reach out to you when serving you with a lawsuit. However, if the agent breaches this request, it is an offense in federal law and can be used as future leverage.

THINGS NOT TO DO

Here are some of the things you should never do when dealing with calls from debt collectors:

1. Don't Provide the Collector with Your Personal Financial Information

While some debt collectors might ask for your personal information claiming that they want to qualify you for a lower payment, doing so might actually be very risky since your information can be used to collect a debt from you if a lender receives a court judgment.

Some of the personal information that you should not disclose to a debt collector include:

- Bank account details
- Social Security number
- Value of property that you own
- Your employer or employment details
- Value or details of any other investment or assets
- Avoid acknowledging old debts

It is okay, however, to provide basic information about your income and the financial problems that you are experiencing. As a general rule of thumb, if you feel that the details you provide could be used to commit an identity theft crime, you should not give it to a collection agency.

2. Refrain from Making Promises

Refrain from making any promises of paying as soon as possible unless you are certain about fulfilling them.

3. Don't Lose Your Cool or Become Abusive

Although dealing with calls from collectors can be a very frustrating process, you should try to maintain a calm demeanor and resist the urge to be rude or abusive towards your debt collectors. If you feel this way, then simply hang up. Otherwise, it could harm your future ability to negotiate the best outcome.

In conclusion, here are some of the main takeaways from this chapter:

- The FDCPA and FCRA are acts that protect debtors against unfair debt collection practices, enforce fairness, accuracy, and the privacy of your information, respectively.
- The avalanche and debt snowball methods are key strategies you can use to identify debts that need more priority
- When dealing with debt collectors, always keep a record of all your documents and debts
- Always set an appropriate time to speak with your debt collectors and tell them if you are unable to speak to them at any time.

- Never disclose your personal information such as an address, bank details, and social security number to debt collectors
- During negotiations, maintain a cool and collected demeanor and refrain from abusing them since they can use this against you if the case goes to court.

CHAPTER FOUR: HOW TO HACK YOUR LOANS

The main reason for most people to consolidate their loans is to reduce the cost of their loan (hence hacking) and thus make the payments affordable. This is achieved by reducing the average interest rate on the debts or at least reducing the payment to an affordable level by increasing the average term of the debts. So, in this chapter, we will look at what loan consolidation is, how it works, its benefits as well as some of the risks associated with it. Finally, I will provide you with some useful tips on how to approach loan consolidation in the right way.

WHAT IS LOAN CONSOLIDATION AND HOW DOES IT WORK?

Loan consolidation involves combining all the debts that you are making separate payments for and obtaining a substantial loan to pay them all at once. In doing so, you essentially bring all the different debts that you owe into a single combined loan for which you make one monthly payment. Debt consolidation is a strategy that is commonly used to consolidate small unsecured loans such as payday loans, credit card loans, overdraft balances, and bills.

Consolidated loans are usually issued by banks, finance companies, and credit unions, and they are typically backed by an asset - *which can be claimed by the lender in case the borrower fails to pay back the loan.* One of the most common ways of consolidating your debts is by obtaining a home equity line of credit or HELOC. This is a loan that you borrow against the equity of your home. Lenders usually allow you to borrow between 85-90% of your home equity which you should pay back within an agreed duration in order to keep your line of credit open. Since a HELOC is a secured loan, defaulting on the payment can result in your property being foreclosed and sold by the lender in order to recoup their money.

While taking a consolidation loan can be a useful strategy, this option also features several risks that can actually hurt your efforts when seeking to get out of debt. It is therefore important to weigh the benefits and the risks before deciding whether this is the right option for you.

BENEFITS OF DEBT CONSOLIDATION

Debt consolidation is a very handy financial tool that can help you to ease your financial burden. Here are some of the advantages of employing loan consolidation as a debt management strategy.

- Lower Interest Rate

One of the disadvantages of servicing multiple loans from different creditors is that you have to pay interest on each of these loans, some of which can be very high. This problem can become even more exacerbated when you miss payments and the interest gets compounded. Taking a consolidation loan allows you to focus on a single interest rate, which is typically lower since the loan amount is large. As a result, you end up making more affordable monthly payments which could allow you to reduce your debt faster.

- Makes it Easier to Manage Payment Deadlines

When you are dealing with multiple creditors with different payment plans and deadlines, it can be very challenging to keep track of your debt payments and avoid defaulting. Also, the penalties for late or missed payment can easily add up.

By consolidating all your smaller debts into a single loan, however, you can manage your payment more efficiently since you only need to make a single monthly payment.

- Regular Fixed Payment

Consolidating all of your debts into a single loan allows you to manage your debt payment better since you are only required to make one regular fixed payment every month instead of multiple monthly payments - which may fluctuate from one month to the next. By taking on a consolidation loan, you no longer have to worry about unexpected bills cropping up every other month. This makes it a lot easier to budget since you only need to set aside a specific amount of money every month to make your monthly payment on your consolidation loan.

- Can Help You to Improve Your Credit

Missing payments or defaulting on loans can significantly hurt your credit score and affect your ability to procure loans at low-interest rates. If you are struggling with multiple loans at the same time, the risk of missing payments is very high since you may not be able to make all payments on time. However, by consolidating your debts into a single loan with a fixed interest rate, you are better able to make payments more comfortably and keep track of your debts so that you do not miss a single payment. In doing so, you will be able to maintain a good credit score, which will help you to secure low-interest loans in the future with relative ease.

RISKS OF LOAN CONSOLIDATION

While loan consolidation can be a great option for better managing your debt, it is not always the best choice, and often comes with several risks which can worsen your financial situation if not mitigated. Understanding the danger of loan consolidation is therefore very important when deciding whether or not to take on a consolidation loan. Some of the risks associated with this process include:

- Sinking into More Debt

One of the biggest dangers of taking a consolidation loan is that you might be tempted to take on new credit without first putting your spending under control. When you secure a consolidated loan to repay your debts, you are able to build your credit on the cards that you have transferred debt from. If you begin taking on new loans from these cards, you will soon end up accumulating more debt in addition to the consolidation loan that you still owe. This can put you in a very difficult financial position since you will suddenly have multiple debts that you need to repay. Since you already have a consolidation loan pending, it will be very difficult *(if not impossible)* for you to obtain a new loan. As a result, you will find yourself in a worse financial situation than you were before.

To mitigate this problem, you should avoid taking a consolidation loan until you get your spending habits under control. If you do take a consolidation loan, pay-off card balances immediately and simultaneously cancel the account and cut up the card. Don't put this off.

- You May End Up Paying More Interest

One of the biggest advantages of consolidation loans is that they help you to cut down on high-interest rates. Personal loans are typically charged lower interest rates compared to credit card and payday loans. However, your interest rate isn't the only factor that determines how much you will end up paying in interest when servicing a loan.

The amount of interest that you incur on a loan also depends to a large extent on the duration of debt repayment. Suppose you take a consolidation loan and reduce your monthly payments by stretching the repayment period, your interest may be lower than what you were paying initially, but since you will make monthly payments for a longer period of time, you may end up paying a higher amount of interest in the long run.

- Risk of Losing Your Home or Retirement

As we mentioned at the outset of this chapter, a consolidation loan is frequently a secured loan, which means it is backed by some kind of collateral. When most borrowers take on consolidation loans, they usually attach their home or retirement fund (401k) to the loan. While this is a great way to secure funds for repaying your debts, doing so is very risky since you may end up losing your home or having a huge percentage of your 401k taken in the event that you default on your monthly payments. You should, therefore, think very carefully about converting your low-risk unsecured loans such as credit cards and payday loans to a consolidation loan which carries a much higher risk.

Moreover, ensure that you bring your spending under control and cancel all your other lines of credit to avoid being in a worse situation a little further down the line. This is what happens to a significant number of people who take this route.

- Getting Lured into a Consolidation Scam

There are plenty of lenders out there who market their debt consolidation loans to struggling consumers who are desperate to get out of debt. However, some of these loans aren't customer friendly. In most cases, they charge very high-interest rates, have very long payment periods, and often attach very exorbitant penalties when a customer misses a payment. Taking on a consolidation loan from such a company can be very frustrating, and will likely keep you in debt for much longer. Even more egregious is the fact that they charge sky-high arrangement fees for the privilege of doing this, thus possibly negating any benefit. I would therefore highly recommend speaking with your local credit union if you choose to go this route.

SECOND MORTGAGES AND HELOC

A second mortgage is a loan that is secured on a home that already has a primary loan. Just like a primary mortgage, a secondary mortgage uses the home as collateral. In the event that you are unable to repay this mortgage, your home may become repossessed by your lender. The home may consequently be sold off in order to repay what you owe.

A home equity line of credit (HELOC) is similar to a secondary mortgage but also functions like a credit card. You can take a HELOC loan to meet financial obligations that you have such as paying for other debts *(loan consolidation)*, purchasing a vehicle, or financing a business.

Both second mortgages and HELOCs are very popular for debt consolidation. The reason for this is that they are very cheap (have low-interest rates) compared to typical unsecured debt that is being consolidated. Therefore your monthly payments are likely to drop substantially. The reason for this is that the lender now has an asset, your house, that is protecting them against you defaulting. Like all secured loans if you don't keep up the payments you risk foreclosure.

When applying for a HELOC, your lender will want to know the amount of equity you have on your home, the appraised value of the home, your income, credit score, and outstanding debts. These details help the lender to determine the value of your collateral as well as your credit risk. Once they have verified your income and conducted an appraisal on the property, your lender will reach out to you and make an offer. If your lender approves your request for the HELOC, they will give you account cards or checks so that you are able to access the loan conveniently.

It is important for you to understand how your HELOC loan works before taking one since terms may vary from one loan to another. While some loans require immediate payment of all the money in a lump sum at the end of the draw period, some may allow you to make payments in installments over an extended duration.

HELOC loans are relatively easy to access if you have a home that can be used as collateral and a good credit score.

However, they pose a major financial risk since you can lose your home if you fail to repay the loan. Taking a HELOC loan can also increase your debt burden if you use it to repay loans without changing your borrowing habits. Before taking one, therefore, you should speak to a financial advisor in order to work out a program that helps you to manage your finances better and get out of debt faster.

BEST APPROACH TO LOAN CONSOLIDATION

Consolidating debt is one way to manage your debt but one that you should be wary of since it can actually leave you worse off financially if you continue with the spending and borrowing habits that have put you in debt in the first place. Loan consolidation usually works best for high-interest loans such as credit card debts and payday loans. However, regardless of the kind of debt that you are trying to pay back, having a solid plan will increase the chances of successfully consolidating your loan without further straining your financial situation.

Let us now look at some of the strategies that you may find beneficial when consolidating a loan.

- Create a Budget

In order to make the most out of your debt consolidation plan, it is absolutely vital that you make a budget. Your basic budget should feature allocations for debt payments, emergency funds as well as saving. In addition to this, you should also account for non-recurring expenses such as car registration in order to avoid piling more debt, which can interfere with your ability to budget.

- Stop Charging Your Credit Cards

One of the most common reasons why loan consolidation often fails for some people is because they use it as an opportunity to borrow even more. Taking a consolidation loan to pay off your credit card loans is likely to improve your credit score and enable you to seek more credit. However, you should be very wary about jumping on this opportunity since charging your credit card after consolidation will quickly lead to more debt. As a rule of thumb, you should cancel all your credit cards and only keep one (usually the oldest) in order to build a good credit score.

- Compare different Consolidation Products

When consolidating your debt, it is always wise to not jump on the first option that you find. Otherwise, you may end up being shortchanged by your provider and be stuck in more debt. For this reason, it is absolutely crucial that you compare interest rates from different lenders as well as other terms that they offer in order to find the consolidation package that is best suited for you. You should ideally source from a lender that sends money directly to your creditors since this will eliminate the temptation to use the consolidation fund for other purposes other than debt repayment.

One of the best ways to source consolidation loans is through credit unions. These are customer-owned cooperatives which are directly controlled by members and designed to provide maximum financial benefit to those members. Credit unions are very advantageous since they offer high-interest rates on deposits and very low-interest rates on loans. Sourcing a consolidation loan from a credit union can therefore allow you to access debt consolidation loans at very reasonable rates compared to banks.

In summary, here are some of the key points to remember from this chapter:

- Loan consolidation involves combining all unsecured loans that you owe to different creditors and obtaining a larger secured loan to repay off all your debts.
- Consolidation allows you to minimize the amount of interest that you pay on multiple loans by combining them into a single monthly payment with a low and stable interest rate.
- In order to successfully consolidate your debt, you will need to change your spending habits as well as make a new budget which accounts for the new loan that you are taking up.
- Cancel all cards, leaving just one if you want to rebuild your credit rating.
- Loan consolidation is far from being an ideal solution to debt management, and should therefore be used only after other avenues have been exhausted.
- Always conduct due diligence when looking for the right consolidation product in order to avoid getting scammed by lenders who charge very high-interest rates and have unfavorable terms of repayment.

CHAPTER FIVE: DEBT MANAGEMENT PLANS

Debt Management Plans are a service offered by nonprofit credit counseling agencies to aid you to return to a debt-free, financially stable life. A financial counselor can also help you determine if entering into a debt management plan (DMP) is appropriate.

A financial counselor (use an NFCC certified agency) will set up a voluntary agreement between you and your creditors. If you sign up for a DMP, you will make a single payment each month to the nonprofit agency who then distributes those funds directly to your creditors. Under this type of debt management program, you could benefit from waived or reduced finance charges or fees, and experience fewer collection calls. When you work with an NFCC agency on a DMP, your accounts are credited with 100 percent of the amount you pay, no charges are deducted. Moreover, by setting a lower monthly payment, it takes the pressure off of your budget and enables you to build your personal savings or even purchase your first home!

However, participating in a DMP won't have a negative effect on your credit score. Although there will be a note on your credit report that says you're enrolled in a debt management plan, it's not something FICO uses when determining a credit score. In fact, DMP can have a positive impact on your credit score. Timely payment history comprises 35% of a FICO credit score, and this will positively impact the score. The decline in the amount you owe, which makes up 30% of the score, will also increase it. Finally, because you are involved in a DMP, there won't be any inquiries for new credit, which is 10% of the score. Opening a lot of new accounts in a short period of time has a negative effect on your score.

In some cases, agencies are able to work with creditors to stop legal action and develop a solution that may satisfy everyone. If you maintain your payment arrangements mostly, the majority of phone calls will stop.

Because each agency uses independently certified consumer credit counselors who will evaluate your total financial position and will help you arrive at realistic solutions to your individual financial problem. Therefore creditors will trust and work with the agency.

HOW DOES A DMP WORK

A DMP puts you in a position to pay off your debts — typically from credit cards — over three to five years. With a DMP, several debts are rolled into one monthly payment and creditors reduce your interest rate. In exchange, you agree to a payment plan that usually runs three to five years. Note that interest rate cuts are standardized across credit counseling agencies, based on your creditors' guidelines and your budget.

DEBT MANAGEMENT PLANS: PROS AND CONS

Pros:

- Consolidates several debts into one payment.
- Could reduce your interest rate by half or more.
- Pays off debt faster than doing it yourself.

Cons:

- Principally for credit card debt. It can't be used for student loans, medical debt, or tax obligations.
- It will take 3 to 5 years.
- You will be unable to use credit cards or get new lines of credit while on the plan.
- Missing a payment can derail the plan and end your interest rate cuts.
- Agencies will charge a small sign up (usually $30 to $40) and then a monthly ongoing fee (typically around $30).

Depending on the agency, only 10% to 20% of clients end up using a debt management plan. From those who do, about 50% to 70% complete the plan.

CONSIDER A DMP IF:

- You have a steady income and think you could pay off your debt within five years if you had a lower interest rate.
- Your unsecured debt, such as from credit cards, is between 15% and 39% of your annual income.

- You can get by without opening new lines of credit while on the plan.

OTHER DEBT MANAGEMENT STRATEGIES TO CONSIDER

Debt Management Plans are not always the best option. Student loans and medical debts will not be covered under such plans. Other options include:

- If your problem debt is less than 15% of your net annual income, you could use the debt avalanche or debt snowball method (see chapter 3).
- A debt consolidation loan (see chapter 4) can also gather debts into one at a lower interest rate if you have good enough credit to qualify. You will also have control over the duration of the loan and hold onto your rights to open new lines of credit.
- Bankruptcy may be better if your debt is more than 40% of your annual income and you see no way to pay it off within five years. This can quickly give you a fresh start, and consumers' credit scores can start to rebound in as little as six months.

HOW TO GET A DMP

If you think a DMP might be your best strategy, then start by choosing a credit counseling agency. Consider certification and accreditation. Look for an agency that's a member of the Financial Counseling Association of America or the National Foundation for Credit Counseling. They both require certification, a standard level of quality among counselors and also require agencies to be accredited by an independent organization.

CHAPTER FIVE: DEBT MANAGEMENT PLANS

Access: Ask yourself how you'd prefer to receive services - over the phone, in person, or online.

Cost: Fees vary by agency, the state you live in, and your financial need. Before you sign up, verify how much you'll pay each month toward your debt and in fees

In summary, here is what you need to know:

- A debt management plan (DMP) allows you to consolidate several debts into one. This can reduce the APR and help you to pay off your debts fast
- Debt settlement plans may not be ideal since they typically mean you'll have to pay off your debts for up to 5 years and you rack up high interest payments in case you fail to make payments on time
- DMPs typically work best for unsecured debts that are between 15% to 39% of your income

CHAPTER SIX: THE SECRETS OF NEGOTIATION THAT YOU MUST KNOW

"The supreme art of war is to subdue the enemy without fighting."

— SUN TZU

THIS CHAPTER IS THE BEATING HEART OF THIS BOOK. WE WILL explore precisely why you should try to renegotiate the terms of your debt, why your lenders might agree, and the associated pre-requisite conditions before you start. Lastly, we will examine the key tools and techniques that will make your negotiation successful. One final word to add here is that it is not only unnecessary but counterproductive to be the type of person who approaches these negotiations as a shouting match and full of aggression. If you are the quiet, thoughtful type, then you can be even more successful, the only requirement is to follow the advice and script, and learn how to say no without saying no.

Finally, before we get started, I would like to thank Chris Voss, the ex FBI hostage negotiator who opened my eyes to what was really possible in negotiation. His book *"Never Split the Difference: negotiate as if your life depended on it"* was the first major step forward in negotiation theory in over a decade since all the theory work going on in academia at that point was based on win-win and "Getting to Yes", but his techniques blew that approach out of the water. These techniques are perfectly suited to ourselves and negotiation with more 'powerful' parties, where our leverage is circumscribed.

Win-win is easy; it saves face, we get half the pie each to be safe. It is driven by fear and to avoid pain. Chris says "creative solutions are almost always preceded by some degree of risk, annoyance, confusion, and conflict." However, in our case, it is also likely to end up in failure as it is based on a dynamic of relatively equal negotiating power.

WHY DO A DEBT RENEGOTIATION

A debt renegotiation is a major opportunity to hit the reset button, not just on your debt, but on your life. What are the alternatives? To stumble on robbing Peter to pay Paul, this type of approach where all of your disposable income gets gobbled up by your creditors? Alternatively, to go nuclear and file for bankruptcy? This will have a similar result, except the main difference is that at least you know you will escape after a few years, and it may many years before you can borrow money again. Perhaps not a bad thing!

The main question you are probably asking right now is: "Tom, what sort of result can I expect to achieve?" This will is not a simple answer; it is very dependent on how delinquent your loans are - delinquent loans are those that are 90 days past due. The best case is that you could literally end up paying 20- 40 cents on the dollar, to achieve this it is optimal if your loans are 150 to 180 days overdue (or DOFD + 60), but before they are charged off (and sold). Lower numbers may be achieved after the debt is very delinquent and has been sold on at least once, but the chances do not necessarily improve, this will depend on the OC. Once debts are time-barred and are no longer enforceable it is possible to settle at a very low level, perhaps 10 cents on the dollar.

One thing to remember is that for unsecured loans, once you stop making the payments, the clock is ticking for the loan companies to collect. Depending on which state (country) you are in will depend on how long they have. Typically after about 6 or 7 years, they can no longer enforce the debt (due to the statute of limitations). However, if you make a payment, the clock starts all over again.

At the other end of the scale, if you are still paying even the minimum payment in full, then your creditor is going to be harder to convince as things are going perfectly fine as far as they are concerned.

HOW NOT TO DO IT.

A client recently came to me for advice, let's call her Sarah. In many ways, her situation was typical. She has student loans, store cards, credit cards, and car loans. However, she had already got herself a budget, cut back on expenses, and had paid off several smaller loans. So far, so good, right? At this point, she realized the biggest loan was going to take years to pay off as she was barely denting the capital. So she rang the credit company to try and negotiate the loan. The conversation, as reported to me, went something like this.

Collections Operator: Hello, XYZ loan company, you are speaking to Julie, how may I help you today?

Sarah: Hi, yes, I am ringing about my loan…

Julie, Collections operator: May I take account reference, and ask some security questions?

[We will skip that part}

Julie, Collections operator: So how can I help you today, Sarah?

Sarah: I am having trouble paying my loan and would like to know if there is something you can do?

Julie, Collections operator: Hi, yes. I see your payments are all up to date? You are making the minimum payments...... [Their favorite type of customer]

Sarah: Can you give me a better rate?

Julie, Collections operator: Let me see what I can do? [silence sound of typing] No, I am sorry that is the best rate for you.[The computer says "no" response]

Sarah: Oh, I was hoping...

Julie, Collections operator: I am sorry it isn't possible. Is there anything else I can help you with today, Sarah?

Sarah: Errr

Julie, Collections operator: You have a nice day... thank you [click]

CREATING CONDITIONS FOR SUCCESS

As we have just seen, there are some minimum conditions for success, and after we meet those, there is scope for major breakthroughs. Before we go further into these conditions, I should point out that if you want to score really deep successes, it is almost certainly necessary to sacrifice your credit score. This can be rebuilt, but if you are going to be squeamish about this, then reduce your leverage to drive a really good bargain. However good our negotiating techniques, we have to remove unbelievability from the negotiation at least. What do I mean? It is not necessary that they really deeply, truly believe everything you say. However, it cannot be obvious, or even very likely to be false, as far as the other party is concerned. This would destroy trust and your negotiating platform with it.

The first step is to create the conditions for negotiation, or at least the pretext. Therefore it is necessary to withhold payment if your loan is not already in arrears. Payments are not reported late to credit bureau for at least 30 days, so bear in mind that it won't affect your credit rating until this point. Also, see the chapter on how to deal with specific types of loans as the risks and exact approach will be different for each. You probably don't want to get your car towed away, or your house repossessed, and we will discuss later how we minimize those risks.

If you want to avoid late payment fines, it would be possible to open the conversation with the fact that you cannot make the next payment, but this will not have the same effect. Otherwise, consider one missed payment the opening shot in the negotiation.

The specific steps to prepare for your successful negotiation are covered in the next chapter. The rest of this chapter will be dedicated to the negotiating approach and how to perform the specific techniques.

WHY WILL CREDIT COMPANIES NEGOTIATE WITH ME?

Earlier in the chapter, I mentioned "win-win" and how we wanted to move beyond that. However, there has to be something in a deal for the other side, otherwise, they either won't agree or won't comply. The whole basis of our approach is to understand the credit company's position and weaknesses and exploit them to our advantage.

What makes creditors more scared than anything else is the fear of a total loss. That is to say, where they have to write off the total balance. This is why once they have failed to collect a loan or enter an arrangement after a period, they will sell the debt on. The longer the debt is not collected then the further it is sold on down the debt collecting food chain.

Debt purchase involves buying the actual debts, including any future interest, along with the right to collect them. These are typically portfolios of mainly unsecured consumer credit loans; or other consumer receivables from companies such as banks, credit card issuers, utilities, or telecoms providers which have billed consumers for having provided a service to them.

This is the fundamental point: at any moment in the process, the owner of your debt will be weighing what they can get from you versus what they can get for selling it in the (debt purchase) market. In theory, this should be their bottom line. However, there are always a few variables such as the future interest stream, especially with credit card debt, which doesn't have a fixed-term or interest rate. Generally, we should consider the current balance owed as their guideline for starting the recovery. For difficult-to-collect debts, collection agencies also negotiate settlements with consumers for less than the amount owed.

From our perspective, the important point from an FTC report in 2013 of more than 3,400 portfolios is this: buyers only paid an average of 4.0 cents per dollar of debt face value. Let me say that again – debt was sold for an average of 4 cents on the dollar! The older debt was sold for a significantly lower price than newer debt. The price of debt older than 15 years was almost zero. Buyers paid the same prices for debt purchased from original creditors and resellers, once the analysis controlled for other observable characteristics of the debt, such as their age and type. Remember that the nominal value of debt will usually include some elements of future interest, especially on personal loans.

Debt purchase agencies also have a long history of using the contract to load the debt with penalty charges for late/non-payment, for collection activities, legal fees, and interest to eye-watering levels to frighten you into paying.

However, their motivation is essentially the same, they will just seek to make a profit on the debt they purchase, or at least no further loss caused by selling it on further.

The answer to the question of why will your creditor negotiate you then is fear that you won't or can't pay. We need to let them convince themselves that you can't pay. Notice that I didn't say you need to convince them – an important distinction is to bend their reality so that they convince themselves, which is more effective. We will be coaxing them to this conclusion and then giving them a way out. The way out is part of what you must decide before the negotiation starts.

EXPLOITING THE EMOTIONAL - AN APPROACH TO NEGOTIATION

"It is self-evident that people are neither fully rational nor completely selfish and their tastes are anything but stable." Kahneman.

We are going to adopt the fundamental techniques of selling to win our negotiation. How do we sell? In this case, we are going to try and get through three steps with the person we are talking to:

1. Establish rapport
2. Gain trust
3. Persuade (tactical empathy)

To achieve this, we are going to exploit the findings of Kahneman and Tversky in their study of cognitive bias in individuals. They found that we are primarily emotional animals, which distorts the way we view the world. Two separate decision-making processes are going on in the brain.

1. Fast, instinctive, and emotional
2. Slow, deliberate, and logical

The key here is that when we think we are using process #2: slow, deliberate, logical; that part of the brain has already been influenced by process #1, which is mostly emotional. We can exploit this in that if we can affect their process #1 thinking – their emotions – then we will guide their system # 2 thinking without them being aware of it.

When we are approaching this negotiation, it is in a different way to what you might expect. You are not pumped up and ready to ram your offer down their throat. Totally the opposite. You are going to be friendly and calm, apologetic that you need to bother them with your problem. Keep your approach friendly, apologetic, and self-deprecating. When you speak, remember to smile, although no one can see you, it will come through in your demeanor and keep you in the right frame of mind.

The approach will help gain their empathy, will make you seem unthreatening, and put them (apparently) in control. This is the key. It is the judo throw of negotiation using their weight and momentum against themselves. If everything goes to plan, they will finish with a warm, fuzzy feeling about themselves, that they have helped a fellow human being.

HOW DO YOU THINK I CAN DO THAT?

The means to go through this process and come out the other side with the solution that we want is to give them your problem to solve. That problem is how do you pay this debt? We want them to come to an answer not to try and provide them with the solution.

What we aim for initially is an opening into the conversation that allows us to ask a carefully calibrated open question

"How do *you* think I can pay for that?" This gets them working on your problem, and ultimately, if we manage it right, they will start to bid against themselves.

You may have to share information about income and other loans in this process, and that is why you need to be prepared (also covered in the next chapter), and reveal only what you want to reveal.

ASSESSING YOUR COUNTERPART

The fundamental part of this negotiation approach is to gain empathy with your counterpart: the poor collections person sitting in some office or soul-less contact center which is doing this 8 hours a day, five days a week.

Chris Voss says that empathy is " the ability to recognize the perspective of a counterpart and the vocalization of that recognition".

Their job is to get the metaphorical blood out of a stone, and they are probably subjected to rudeness and abuse on a regular basis. They have probably also heard every artificial sob story ever. Therefore, adopting a friendly and empathetic approach will create openings.

Suppose we were to consider that these employees will generally fall into one of two types. Either they don't like their job and find pressuring people to pay money they don't have stressful, or they will be hardass types who consider debtors to be feckless scroungers who shouldn't have borrowed money they couldn't repay.

The former type will be more easily influenced as it will be more straightforward to gain their trust. But in either event, you must listen carefully and try to assess the person at the other end of the phone. The more you know about someone, the more power you will have in the negotiation.

When they are initially retrieving your information, try to get in some general questions to find openings. They will be half distracted by retrieving and reading information.

You can say something like " I bet this is a tough job?" or "Has it been a rough/ long day today?" or a more neutral "I expect you had a lot of calls already today – how do you handle it all?"

Then this can be followed by "I don't' know how you manage if people are angry or abusive." This will stir their emotional pot.

You can finish the exchange with " I expect you get lots of people like me who get in over their heads." Planting a seed of the view that you want to cultivate.

YOUR OPENING STATEMENT

At some point, after they have retrieved your details, usually they will ask how they can help, what it is you want. This initial opening is crucial to getting on the right track. We want to exploit their offer of help and make them do the work, not provide answers. First, however, we need to give them a reason and to set the scene.

So your opening has to run something along the lines of:

"I am afraid I have got into debt over my head and find that I can't pay any longer."

You will have to provide a reason that triggered the change. I would avoid lying where possible. Here are some reasons:

- I / my wife/husband/partner just lost my / their job
- As above but (we) were forced to take a pay cut

- Our business has dropped off a cliff since COVID because….[we work in travel]
- I / my wife/husband/partner got sick and we are paying for treatment and medical bills
- My parents were helping us/me out but they just got sick/ made redundant.

The next part of the conversation will depend on your offer and whether you want to try to settle it or negotiate better terms, and how many creditors you have. If you can convince them you can't pay, then one of the points of leverage is threatening to use what money you have to pay someone else, leaving them with nothing. We will discuss these approaches in the next chapter as I want to turn now to how you manage and control the negotiation using different tools.

5 ACTIVE LISTENING TECHNIQUES

I am now going to outline the 5 critical techniques that you are going to use to generate rapport, which will build trust, which will allow you to influence the result.

What you are applying here is a toolbox for active listening – this is not a passive activity you are reacting all the time to what the other person says.

"To quiet the voices in *your* head, make your sole and all-encompassing focus the other person and what they have to say." Chris Voss - *Negotiating as if your life depended on it*.

MIRRORING

Mirroring is the technique of repeating back the last three keywords used by your counterpart. By repeating their own words back to them, they will feel that you have understood and internalized what they are saying. They will, in turn, feel that you are on the same wavelength as them. This is a similar technique to adopting the same body language as your interlocutor in a face to face situations. It builds rapport.

For example, they say, "I see that your last payment was in June and your account is 60 days past due." If you mirror this back "60 days past due", it demonstrates to them that you hear them and you are listening intently.

It is a more powerful technique than it may sound, it sounds straightforward and perhaps fake, but it is very important to building the rapport, and should not be underestimated.

Try it with your partner or spouse or spouse for a while to practice. They will subconsciously notice and that you are more attentive, and you may begin to feel a difference in your relationship.

SILENCES – EFFECTIVE PAUSES

The purpose of using silence, not responding to a statement or request, is to pressure the other party into filling the void. They will feel the need to continue speaking and thus are likely to reveal more information than they intended. This could be about how they are thinking and feeling, not just facts.

The power of silence comes from the fact that most people, especially extroverts, are just not comfortable with silence, especially in phone conversations where there are no other mediums to substitute. Therefore, people feel immense psychological pressure to continue speaking.

The converse is also true. Once you have made a point or statement, do not feel tempted to over-elaborate. This just makes you seem weaker and less confident and you may go on to reveal something you didn't intend to.

If they make a statement, you can simply respond with minimal encouragement. For example, you would say "I see", or " Yes", or "Uh-huh" this puts the ball back in their court to continue and elaborate. This pressure can make them start to negotiate with themselves in an effort to fill the space.

Think about it another way. Who do you trust more, the fast-talking salesperson who doesn't shut up to let you think of the person who gives you the space to make your own decision? The second person will appear to be listening to you more, so will appear more trustworthy. Remember, our goal is to build that trust, so we can influence others.

Also, remember that you can't make a mistake or let something slip if they are talking. The person doing the listening is the person in control of a conversation. This doesn't mean you should say nothing if they make a statement you disagree with. We will look at ways to say no without saying no in a moment – and why it is advantageous.

Again practice on your partner or in other conversational settings by using just encouragers to keep the conversation going. Become comfortable with being with people and being silent.

THE POWER OF GIVING OBJECTIONS A NAME - LABELING

This technique is the hardest to learn because to apply it, you must identify the other parties underlying objections/emotions and then be able to respond by labeling them. The importance of this particular approach is that giving the objection or the emotion a name allows the other person's mind to process and then sidestep the issue.

For example, if you said, "It seems like you are feeling

angry?" then the very act of attaching the label of anger to the emotion allows the other party to recognize it for what it is, and process (get over) the emotion. They realize that you know they are angry, and thus it allows them to move on: they no longer need to feel angry. Otherwise, they will continue to feel angry but without being able to place it.

This is how it works in terms of the brain. You can reduce the negative impact of feelings by giving them a name and increase your acceptance and understanding. When you experience any strong emotion, your amygdala becomes active – this is the part of the brain that processes emotion. The amygdala triggers a wave of physical reactions in your body, like increased sweating, anxiety, increased heart rate, and so forth. When you attach a label to the emotion, the frontal cortex (analytical part of the brain) kicks in to process it, and the amygdala calms down.

A study by UCLA's Social Cognitive Neuroscience Laboratory showed how this works. Subjects were connected to an MRI machine, which monitors brain activity. When the subjects were shown, photographs of faces expressing strong emotions, their amygdalas became active. When they were asked to label the emotion they saw in the picture, the amygdala became calmer.

So, if things are becoming a bit tense and agitated, you might say: "It seems like you are worried that your supervisor might not be able to accept this deal." This could cut to the heart of their concern and force it into the open, where they can process what to do about their boss. On the other hand, labeling can be as straightforward as saying, "it seems like you had a difficult day today".

Lastly, you can also use labeling as a form of flattery. "It seems like you're the sort of person who…."

- Gets results

- Is good with people / understands people
- Prides themselves on being fair.

PARAPHRASING AND SUMMARIES, GETTING: "THAT'S RIGHT".

In his book, Chris Voss says that the words you want to hear in a negotiation are, "That's right!"

If you get "yes" from your counterpart, it could actually mean several things: compliance, or I agree with, but I am not committed, or even be a counterfeit yes. As in, I'll back out later under some pretext. However, he says that when you hear "That's right" it means that you have convinced your counterpart in the negotiation that you have heard and understood them and that they start to trust you. It is far more meaningful and powerful than yes.

Once you hear "That's right!" it means they are ready to move on in the negotiation from some sticking point and to hear and agree to your proposal. They have emptied the emotion and believe you have gained empathy. It created a realization point with our adversary when they decided on a point without the feeling of giving in. It's a stealth victory, and they embrace it.

There are two techniques for drawing a "that's right" from your opposite party. The first method is to paraphrase. Take what they have said in the last couple of statements and then regurgitate it in your own words in a more condensed form.

Again, this achieves empathy and trust as replaying their thoughts without judgments will demonstrate you have been listening and absorbing their perspective.

The second method is a bit similar but comes into play when discussions have been lengthier or more extended, and points have been made over more time. You simply summarise the other side's negotiating position for them, including any labels attached to specific underlying reasons. You may also use mirroring phrases. When they hear this played back to them accurately, they will be inclined to give you a "that's right" response.

To produce an accurate summary apply the following guidelines:

- Delete irrelevant or trivial information.
- Delete redundant information.
- Select the key points.
- Provide labels.
- Use mirroring phrases

CALIBRATED QUESTIONS: SAYING NO WITHOUT SAYING NO

The next and one of the most important techniques in negotiating is the ability to use very open-ended questions. Chris Voss calls these calibrated questions. Calibrated questions often have no target for your opponent to object to. The question is directed, so it aims to elicit their help in solving or answering the question, rather than you putting a counterpoint that can be disagreed with.

" They educate your counterpart on what the problem is rather than causing conflict by *telling* them what the problem is" Chris Voss

The forms of questions are usually who, what, where, when, why, and how. Do not use forms such as can, do, and "are" as most of these can be answered very simply with a yes or no or are not valid. The two preferred forms of calibrated questions are "how" and "what" as these questions cannot usually be answered simply, and your opponent's brain will immediately be opened up trying to solve them. Furthermore, playing dumb and I don't understand are also valid techniques and can buy time for you.

When using calibrated questions, pay attention to your voice to ensure that the tone of voice is requesting help. How can I help you make this better for us? How would you like me to proceed? How can we solve this? How am I supposed to do that? Control your emotions when confronted with an unpleasant demand or statement. Without control of your emotions, you can't control the negotiation. Use a calibrated question to diffuse their position. Hostage mentality is a reaction to a loss of control so that you become hostage to your own emotions instead of being able to engage.

The benefit of using a calibrated question is that it doesn't directly challenge the other party but gets them engaged in solving your problem, which in turn results in them potentially starting to negotiate with themselves and break down their own position to move towards yours.

Another benefit of this approach is that it is an excellent way to say no without saying no. When confronted with a situation where the other side's demands are quite unpalatable you use two or three different types of calibrated questions one after the other to effectively block their request without actually saying no.

For example, if you have explained why you cannot pay, then during the course of the negotiation, they come back with "We think you can pay $343 per month". You would respond with, "How am I supposed to do that?" They now have to engage with you on a complex interaction around how you can implement that.

Remember, during all interactions to be positive and smiling, and this will help maintain the right tone of voice and give a trustworthy impression.

SLOW IT DOWN – MAKE THEM IMPATIENT

Your counterpart likely has some sort of time pressure on them. Either to get a result, get to the next call, or even to go home. Use that as leverage. The power of deadlines is due to fear of future loss, but mostly it is artificial. I have lost track of the number of times I have been told if you sign the contract before the end of the quarter, we can give you this price but only until then. Once an offer is on the table, I have never known it to be successfully taken back.

If you allow the variable of time to trigger such thinking, you have taken yourself hostage creating an environment of reactive behavior and poor choices where your counterpart can now kick back and let an imaginary deadline and your reaction to it do all the work for him.

If you slow it down by using lots of calibrated questions, summaries, paraphrasing, and all the other active listening techniques we have discussed, your opponent will become more impatient for a result. This can be turned to your advantage. Ask to go over things again to ensure you have understood and then turn the screw a bit more. Remember, no deal is better than a bad deal.

ACCUSATION AUDITS

Use what we call an accusation audit early in the negotiation to disarm your opponent. In an accusation, you bring out and state all their objections to your proposal. For example:

"I expect you think I am just a feckless scrounger, who never intended to pay back the money, I suspect you think I am just smoking and drinking away all my income. I am just managing to put basic meals on the table for my children, and I don't smoke or drink. You might think that somehow I can pay these loans, perhaps I should get a third job to pay them….."

By getting all their arguments onto the table at the beginning they cannot use them as leverage later.

BEND THEIR REALITY

> "Bend their reality, so it conforms to what we want to give them, not what they think they deserve."
>
> — CHRIS VOSS

The final point I would like to make on negotiation is that the idea of building rapport, gaining trust is to influence. Once you have done these things and your counterpart feels like they trust you, then you are ready to 'bend their reality'. This means that what they would have seen as a ridiculous outcome at the start of the negotiation they will now be thrilled with. You have moved their whole frame of reference during the negotiation.

The F-Word - FAIR. It's a bomb: "I just want what's fair". Use this judiciously. It is quite powerful and will trigger feelings of defensiveness and discomfort. Conversely, they might try "We have given you a fair offer!"

You are attempting to frame your vision as the perfect solution. Anchor all their emotions in preparation for a loss they will seek to avoid. We naturally try to avoid losses more strongly than we will seek gains. i.e. Say "I will use the money from my parents to pay another lender instead."

Here are the key takeaways from this chapter:

- When negotiating with creditors, use techniques

such as paraphrasing and effective silences to show your opponent that you are listening to them.
- Use accusation audits to disarm your opponent during the negotiation and make them more receptive to your point of view.
- Slow down the negotiations with calibrated questions and summaries to heighten your opponent's anxiety and make them more impatient for a conclusion.
- Always try to show empathy while also being firm with your creditors and make them understand that you are willing to walk away if you do not get the outcome you are looking for.

CHAPTER SEVEN: HOW TO GET WHAT YOU WANT IN JUST 3 STEPS

When it comes to controlling debt, knowing how to negotiate with your creditors can be a priceless asset. Negotiating with your lenders can help you to reach a reasonable settlement plan and avoid negative outcomes such as wage garnishments, bank levies, and foreclosures. Before you initiate negotiations with your creditors, therefore, it is important to understand the strategies that work in order to increase your chances of success. In this chapter, I am going to share with you a 3-step approach on how to get what you want when negotiation with creditors. Although before we start looking at that you need to know how to handle the actual bargaining part. Once you have established rapport, built empathy, and gained trust to bend their reality it will come to the nitty-gritty negotiation.

HOW TO NEGOTIATE WITH CREDITORS - THE ACKERMAN METHOD

The Ackerman Method is a bargaining system that was developed by Mike Ackerman. This model can be applied in a wide array of situations, including bargaining when shopping for everyday items and hostage negotiations. The premise of this model is very simple. You have a target price that you want to arrive at. Once you have determined that price, you want to begin your negotiation with a price that is 65% of your target price. The idea is to make three raises, which will eventually get you to the target price that you have set. Your first increment should be 20%, the second 10%, and the last one 5%. With each raise, you are cutting down the increment by half.

When you get to the final figure, you can throw out an odd number and also throw in a non-monetary object to give the other person the impression that they've tapped you out and you can't go any further. This makes them finally capitulate to your final number, and you end up saving more money than you would otherwise pay. So, let us suppose that your target price is $20,000. The first thing you would need to do is to set your anchor price, which should be about 65% of the amount you are willing to offer. In this example, this would be $13,000.

This price is likely to get a strong reaction from the party that you are negotiating with, but that shouldn't phase you at all. The idea here is to devalue the other party's perception of the item's worth. However, when setting your anchor price, you should be careful not to offend the other person *(by having the price too low)* since this is likely to put them off and possibly cause them to walk out of the negotiation. On the other hand, if the figure is quite reasonable, they will probably engage with you and start bargaining by stating some facts about the item in an effort to make you raise your bid.

Once you have established that the other party is responsive to your bid and open to negotiations, then hopefully they will make a counter offer. Eventually, after saying no without saying no, and using the other techniques we discussed in the last chapter you can raise your anchor amount to 85% *(increase it by 20%)*. Doing so will lure them and make them start warming up to your offer. Do not raise your offers too readily, make them work for it. If they give you a counter, raise your offer to 95 % *(an increase of 10%)* and finally follow up with a rise of 5% to achieve the 100% target price that you had in mind initially. Do not be afraid to walk away between these steps and come back later. Remember also that any time you don't get an outright no, then you are making progress.

The Ackerman Method is very powerful and can yield fantastic results if you know how to apply it correctly. There are two things that you need to ensure when employing this negotiation strategy. First, do not let their anchor price throw you off balance and cause you to change your strategy. Second, make sure your opponent understands that you are willing to walk away if you get a raw deal. If you feel trapped in the negotiation, you are much more likely to become intimidated and capitulate to their demand or offer. So, if you happen to feel pressured during the bargaining process, you should request your opponent for a break so that you can recollect yourself and become grounded again before proceeding with the negotiation.

MISTAKES TO AVOID WHEN NEGOTIATING WITH CREDITORS

When it comes to negotiating with creditors, there are several pitfalls that you need to avoid in order to get the best outcome. These include:

- Not Knowing Whether Your Debt is Secured or Unsecured

As we have seen from the introductory chapter of this book, there are two main types of debt, namely: secured and unsecured debt. Secured debt is any kind of debt that is backed by a physical asset such as a house, car, or retirement fund. If you default on this debt or are unable to pay, your lender has the right to claim the asset that you have attached to your loan. On the other hand, unsecured debt is any kind of debt that is only backed by the promise of the debtor to pay back. In this case, a creditor cannot put a claim on your assets if you fail to pay back the debt.

Some unsecured creditors often attempt to convince their borrowers that a debt is secured and threaten to repossess their assets if they are unable to pay. Understanding whether your debt is secured or unsecured can help you to avoid falling into this trap.

- Ignorance about Your Creditors' Strengths

Creditors of secured loans usually have a number of strengths that they can fall back on when a debtor is unable or unwilling to settle what they owe them. In most cases, secured creditors have the right to repossess your asset in case you default on your loan repayment. Unsecured creditors, on the other hand, do not have this prerogative, but this does not mean that there is no recourse available to them. Some of the options that they may pursue in the event that you fail to pay what you owe include:

1. Calling and Sending Letters

Throughout the process, your lenders will spontaneously call you and send letters demanding payment. You should therefore be adequately prepared to deal with such without losing your composure and/or saying things that you may end up regretting. Do not give away any information that may be of value to the creditor and that can be used to apply (emotional) pressure - stick only to your prepared story/reasons why you cannot pay.

2. Filing a Lawsuit

If your creditor feels that you are unable or unwilling to pay back what you owe them, they are at liberty to sue you even when negotiations are still on-going. Do not let this phase you unduly.

3. Wage Garnishment

In case a creditor wins a lawsuit against you, they can be granted a court order, which allows them to garnish your wages through your employer in order to recoup what you owe them. Never reveal or even confirm your employment details.

4. Bank Account Levies

If your lender wins a lawsuit against you, they may also be awarded the right to withdraw money from your bank account. It is therefore important to keep your bank account balance and refrain from making deposits in your account pending negotiations in order to avoid losing your personal funds and savings. Keep money in prepaid cards and e-money accounts, these are harder to identify or seize

- Not Knowing a Creditor's Weaknesses

Both secured and unsecured creditors typically have a number of weaknesses, which you can use to your advantage when you are in debt. These include:

1. They are Subject to Debt Collection Laws

Debt collection companies are typically subject to compliance laws that are outlined in the Fair Debt Collection Practices Act (FDCPA). This act limits the tactics that debt collectors are allowed to use when collecting a debt.

2. Lawsuits are Expensive

Creditors usually pursue litigation only as a final resort when everything else fails. This is because lawsuits often consume a lot of time and finances, yet ultimately there is no guarantee that the lender will get back their money. Lawsuits can be resisted by finding administrative flaws in the creditor's case and filings.

- Paying too Much

For unsecured loans, creditors are often willing to take pennies on the dollar when it comes to a debt settlement negotiation. However, most debtors do not often realize this, and as a result, end up paying more than they are able to. When negotiating a debt settlement with your creditors, therefore, you should start at a lower figure and aim for 40% or less as the final settlement amount.

Let us now go over a three-step approach that can help you to pursue successful debt repayment negotiations with your creditors.

Step 1: Be Prepared

Before entering any negotiation process with your creditors, it is important to make the necessary preparations. This typically involves gathering all correspondence and material that is related to your debt and the negotiations that you intend to get into.

The first thing you need to be aware of before you begin negotiations is the type of debt that you are dealing with. As we have seen from the previous section, secured and unsecured debts are typically handled differently. Depending on the kind of debt that you owe, they are several options that are available to you as well as various kinds of recourse that your lenders may pursue in order to get their money back. For instance, secured debts are typically backed by physical assets such as homes, vehicles, retirement savings, etc. Your creditors may have your asset foreclosed or repossessed. On the other hand, unsecured debts are not backed by any collateral, so creditors cannot make any claim on your assets if you fail to repay them.

Most likely is that your creditor will take you through a prepared script of monthly budget and expense questions. You have to be able to show you can afford your basic needs and still pay them the agreed amount, even if at zero interest. If not, they are not going to offer you a plan. In this case, you should aim for a settlement. You also do not want to show that you can afford the basics, their payments, and still have several hundred dollars of "walking around" money. They will not offer either their best deal or a settlement.

When preparing for negotiations with creditors, it is also vital to have records of your financial position as well as any correspondence that you had with other creditors. Moreover, you need to ensure that you have your credit report - *you will need to make an order from a credit reporting company such as Experian, TransUnion, or Equifax.* A credit report is essentially a document that helps lenders to determine your credit risk, in other words, how likely you are to make your monthly debt payments on time. Some of the details that are included in your credit report include:

- The date you opened your accounts or took out a loan
- The amount of money available in each account
- Your payment history
- Your credit limits and total loan amounts
- Bankruptcies and liens
- Your identity details including name, address, and social security number

When reading your credit report, you need to ensure that all the data contained in the 'Identifying Information' section actually pertains to you and not someone else who shares your name. You should also confirm that the addresses of all the places you have lived are included in the credit report.

Moreover, double-check the 'Credit History' section to make sure that everything listed there is accurate. Be on the lookout for accounts that seem unfamiliar and payments that have been wrongly listed as late when they in fact are not. It is also vital to ensure that no account has been opened without your consent since this can be a sign of identity theft.

When preparing your negotiations, you should always have a clear objective in mind - *figure out the outcome that you want to achieve out of the settlement negotiation.* This could be an extension of the term of the loan or a reduction in the cost of interest. Knowing what you want out of the negotiation will enable you to prepare your statement and get what you want out of the settlement.

Once you have identified your objective, you need to come up with a story to convince your creditors why you are in your current financial situation and the reason why you are unable to repay the debt as you had intended. The better your creditor understands your situation, the easier it will be for them to agree to a settlement. Furthermore, you need to identify the leverage that is available to you in the negotiations and make sure the other party understands that you are willing to use it to get what you want. This could be anything from challenging the legitimacy of the loan in court or filing for bankruptcy, which inevitably means your creditor won't get anything from you.

It is also important to identify any leverage that your creditor may have. Depending on the kind of debt you are dealing with *(secured or unsecured)*, there are a number of options that your creditors can pursue in case you are unable to pay back what you owe them. For instance, they can choose to file a lawsuit and seek the garnishment of your wages or foreclose and repossess your assets. Being aware of your creditors' potential recourse will aid you in knowing which *buttons* to push and red flags to *avoid* during the negotiation.

Step Two: Map Out the Call

In this step, you will make a plan for how you are going to control the call.

Please remember that the negotiating script is a suggested template that you will need to adapt to your situation. You also need to be ready to respond to the flow of the negotiation. Once you have done one or two, your execution will become more confident and accomplished. This script is based on settling a debt. If you wish to reduce your payment, then adjust at the appropriate points of making an offer. Remember, without a reduction in the interest rate, anything else is meaningless. You are just paying for longer and may pay more in total.

The call script is based on employing the following techniques that we discussed in chapter 6, and is structured as follows:

- No oriented question
- Accusation audit
- A statement that leaves only that's right
- Calibrated questions
- More No oriented questions
- Label flattery
- Ackerman method negotiation: offers of 65 – 85 – 95 – 100% , non-monetary offer

Based on their responses to control the negotiation

- Pauses – slow it down
- Labeling and mirroring answers that are not acceptable
- Calibrated questions

These are the key things that you must add/populate into the script.

Accusation audit	3 - 4 statements based on labeling (It seems)
Reasons why you can now settle (assuming that is your solution) **or other option** (e.g. reduced interest)	
65% Offer	2-4 Prepared calibrated questions to say no
85% Offer	2-4 Prepared calibrated questions to say no
95% Offer	2-4 Prepared calibrated questions to say no
100% offer (and a non-monetary thing, if applicable)	Ensure this is a precise but odd number (e,g, $23,423)

This table and the script template are available for download via my website (so that you can populate and adjust) at www.PersonalFinanceWizard.com

THE DEBT SETTLEMENT CALL – SCRIPT

Put on your biggest smile before dialing!

YOU: "I'm calling to calling to discuss my account [or debt]"
....

- While they are retrieving your information, try to establish rapport.
- Ask some questions, here are some suggestions:
- What state/city are you from? I thought I recognized your accent? [their response] I am from there/ have relatives/ friends/ someone I work with....
- If you work or worked in finance or a call center mention this. Say how you find it.
- If you have student loans use this to ask about theirs. Did they go to the same college, study similar stuff?
- Create an opening to talk about pets. Say your cat or dog jumped up/ came in. Ask if they have any pets.
- Have there been any recent public holidays? Ask about what they did? Are they religious and if so how do they likely view debt and interest?
- Has it been a long shift, when do you go home? …. Sympathize as appropriate.

Only when they finally move the conversation on: give them your background story about why you can no longer pay this debt. (This must tie-in with the information they have on file because you should have had this conversation and given this story earlier in the process)

YOU: "I am afraid I have got into debt over my head and find that I can't pay any longer because....."

CHAPTER SEVEN: HOW TO GET WHAT YOU WANT IN JUST 3 STEPS

- **Finish your opening statement with a no oriented question:**

YOU: "*You were happy to lend me money, now I hit bad times it seems like you don't care what position you are leaving me in?*

In your job that you must hear sob stories every hour of every day that your stock of sympathy is exhausted?

It seems that you want to leave me no choice but to walk away from this debt?"

Let them give their 'no' response to each point

- **Accusation audit (getting their objections in first):**

YOU: "*It seems that you may feel I got myself into these situations and that I deserve it? It seems you think that I want to be in this position and that I engaged in reckless borrowing?* "

After their response

YOU: "*It seems like you are the sort of person who [values the company's reputation/get's results/understand people/pride themselves on being fair]*"

- **Getting That's right**

YOU: "*How do you [or name them: Chase bank/ Bank of America etc.] price debts that can't be paid?*"

Listen very carefully here. Ask them what they will do if you don't pay for 90/120/150/180 days as appropriate. When will they sell the debt? If you hear information to your advantage that would mean waiting, don't be afraid to terminate the call. Try to establish the limit of their authority; if it is too low get the call escalated. Ideally, this should confirm what you already know, as it is a good idea to get this information earlier, so you know what you are working with to calibrate your offer.

When you have extracted maximum information, then give them the "That's right" line. Paraphrase what they just told you, concentrating on the main points and the information most advantageous to you. You should hear "That's right" at the end of the summary.

- **Employ the Ackerman method**

YOU: "So I called today because [my parents/some friends/relatives] [lent/gave/left] me some money that means I can make one of my creditors an offer today to settle my/our debt. I have $xxxxxx [based on 65% of your target settlement according to the Ackerman method] as a one-time settlement in full, including any payment charges. [PAUSE and WAIT for their counter offer]

YOU: *"How do you expect me to do/pay that?"* {remember: to use an upward inflection, not an aggressive tone, sound more surprised}.

Be ready to make a point about paying someone else, or just walking away, reiterate about time-limited nature.

Use more no-oriented questions e.g. how could I get that? Rather than go straight to your next offer.

Step Three: Negotiate hard

After you have mapped out the call, the final thing you need to do is to reach out to your creditor and negotiate the settlement. Try to smile and maintain a calm demeanor throughout the call to establish a comfortable atmosphere for your creditors and make them receptive to your settlement offer. Use the Ackerman method to get what you want out of the negotiation and reach a final settlement. When negotiating with your creditors, the settlement that you finally arrive at will be a verbal one. This will stipulate the amount of money that should be paid *(all at once or in multiple installments)* over a certain period of time until the debt is fully settled. However, just because you have reached a verbal settlement does not mean that the deal is sealed. A settlement is not complete until it has been documented in writing and paid in full according to the terms of the agreement.

The creditor must send you a debt settlement letter, which should include the following details:

- The names of the creditor/debt collector
- The date when the settlement letter was drafted
- Your name
- Your account number
- The bank account balance (although this is not always necessary)
- The agreed settlement amount (this is typically lower than the owed amount)
- The terms of payment and duration when the agreed amount should be cleared
- The date(s) when the payment should be received

In addition to these crucial details, the settlement letter will also include some general information such as disclosures about the debt payment. Your creditors or debt collectors will include these in the settlement letter in order to cover themselves. It is important to note that large banks will generally not provide you with a settlement letter unless your payment arrangements have been registered in their computer systems. Instead, they will ask you to provide them with specific ACH or electronic payment information first, which you will do over a phone call.

Do not pay over any settlement until you receive written confirmation of the agreement, as above.

Here are some of the general rules of thumb that you should adhere to when it comes to a debt settlement:

1. Only make settlement payments from bank accounts that you have specifically set up for the purpose of funding the agreement
2. In case your creditor does not send you the settlement letter within 72 hours of when your payment is supposed to be processed, call and demand to be faxed/emailed the same or the funds will not be available in your account
3. Always be prepared to walk away from a settlement if you don't receive the settlement letter on the day that payment is supposed to be made
4. If you suddenly decide to pull out of a settlement deal, make sure there are no funds in the account designated for payment to avoid losing your money.

Even if you opt to use a debt settlement company or third party negotiator, you should never compromise when it comes to receiving settlement agreements and having the documentation before payment is made.

Keep all documentation regarding the settlement and the payment. It is common for debts to be sold on after settlement and for a new CA to pop up demanding the original amount owed plus additional interest and charges even after the debts are time-barred.

I am choosing this point of the book to point out that if you are successful in getting debt relief by negotiating a settlement, the lender is obliged to notify the IRS, and if IRS finds the total of all write-offs exceed $600, then it will be treated as income.

In summary, here are some of the key points to remember when it comes to debt payment negotiations and repayment:

- The Ackerman Method is a powerful negotiation tool that can help you get the best deal when it comes to debt settlement negotiations
- Before entering into any negotiations with your creditors make sure you do your due diligence to understand the kind of debt you're dealing with *(secured and unsecured)* as well as the strengths and weaknesses of your creditors in order to know the right way to handle it
- Make sure that the verbal agreement is backed by a written settlement letter to avoid getting a raw deal from your creditors.
- Ensure you have the debt settlement letter in your possession before releasing any funds from your dedicated account for debt repayment.
- Keep (forever) any and all documentation relating to the settlement and final payment to avoid the debt coming back to life.

CHAPTER EIGHT: FIGHTBACK USING REPUDIATION

THIS CHAPTER IS PERHAPS THE MOST CONTROVERSIAL IN THE book as it looks at some "non-conformist" methods of clearing your debt, which at the very least will test your determination and destroy your credit rating.

Repudiation means to deny or to push back. Essentially what we propose is to resist our creditors at every turn and try to thwart them by every legal means at our disposal. This is essentially the debt cleanse method, as proposed by Jorge P Newbery, Founder of American Homeowner Preservation LLC, in his book; Debt Cleanse. Notably, this is not a review of the book but we will borrow some of his practices, and I will throw in a few of my own tips myself.

Additionally in this chapter, we will look at how you can go about fighting creditors, credit agencies, and others through the legal process to prevent the process from reaching court, getting a judgment in your favor, and where it goes against you how to protect your assets as best as possible.

Before traveling this route it is worth considering whether going full nuclear and going for bankruptcy would be a better option for you. We will discuss the various bankruptcy options in the final chapters. Finally please remember I am not necessarily advocating an either-or approach, but more of a mix and match. The Debt Cleanse method is about softening up your creditors so that they will negotiate and settle for a fraction of the debt value, so it really works hand in hand with the previous chapters on negotiating.

A LITTLE BACKGROUND

America, despite being the world's richest nation, is a vastly indebted state. Apart from the ever ballooning federal government debt that eclipses the GDP, the U.S is also the country with the most indebted people in the world. Some estimates put the number of Americans with debts, or some form of credit to be 80% of the population, which basically means that almost every adult has a loan. Indeed, we have seen in previous chapters how high the uptake of mortgages, car loans, and student loans is and have discussed specific ways of dealing with each.

Sadly enough, the individual debt burdens are increasing at a supersonic rate courtesy of the 'debt-grooming' strategy of many lending institutions that have made taking loans even for unnecessary expenditures look cool. How many ads have you seen on the big screen assuring you that you can own your dream car even when you don't have the full cash amount at hand? That you can get that family mansion you've always dreamt of by taking a homeowner's loan? Notably, I'm not here to lecture you or judge your reasons for taking a loan. On the contrary, I understand and empathize with how easy it is to get trapped in the bottomless debt abyss and I will walk with you to find a long-lasting solution.

In previous chapters, the focus was on managing and

minimizing your debt burden without messing up your finances and credit score. This chapter looks at what you can do when you are drowning in so much debt that even otherwise effective methods like refinancing, negotiation, and better budgeting won't help you and a bad credit score is the least of your worries. If you consistently go down the route proposed in this chapter and things go against you then you will end up unrated. You need to accept this as a probable outcome.

WHAT IS THE DEBT CLEANSE APPROACH?

Newbery's approach to having unaffordable debt is not to renegotiate them, or even declare bankruptcy, but to not repay them at all. Once you stop paying, then you should keep all the repayments that you would have made to settle debts at a fraction of their value. He proposed to not take your creditor's calls when the due date passes and goes as far as saying you should block their numbers. That's it, don't sit down with them or give them any explanation - just go missing. The idea here is to wear down the lender and make them incur high recovery expenses such that they stop chasing you or at least delay the inevitable long enough to allow you to put your house in order.

If your lender sends you a demand letter, write back disputing the debt agreement terms and if possible, have a specialist debt lawyer help you with that. Scrutinize every letter, email, or text sent by the sender and look for any inconsistencies and legal deficiencies therein and then consult with your attorney on the best way to capitalize on that. If a creditor can make your life hell because of an unpaid loan, you sure as hell can return the favor. As Newbery states, when you are neck-deep in debt, you have nothing to lose, except your fears.

Step 1 - Prepare: Cover All Loopholes and Protect Your Assets

You know by now that when you fall out with your creditors, they will automatically come for your earnings and assets with a view of not only recovering their principal but also leave you poorer as a way of teaching you a lesson. But as Newbery says in the book, the foundation of the Debt Cleanse Approach is the loss of fear or any feelings of embarrassment. Whether your lenders are hauling you to court, or sending ferocious collectors after you, don't show them any fear or subservience. Instead, be firm and arrogant (without being rude), and openly tell them to stop wasting their time.

As you do that, however, you need to have measures in place to protect your core assets from the marauding collectors and their auctioneers. These steps need to be performed as part of the pre-cleanse: before you stop paying all your debts. Here are some of the legal paths you can follow to this effect:

1. Transfer Your Land Ownership to A Trust Fund - This is one of the oldest tricks in the book and is commonly employed by rich folks evading both creditors and the taxman. Basically, you establish a relationship with a land trust board, where they agree to hold your land title for you while you still get to keep the ownership and other benefits of the land. Alternatively create your own trust, especially using offshore entities, and transfer the assets to the trust. That way, your name won't appear on any public records as a landowner, which in turn means your creditors won't pursue you with a view of selling your property.

You can't do this with your average piece of real estate that has a mortgage. The mortgage or any other lien will prevent the transfer of ownership, as the title will show the mortgage/lien.

2. "Sell" Your Car if you own it - As soon as you make up your mind to do a Debt Cleanse, find someone you trust (whether a trusted friend or a close family member) then transfer your car's ownership to them for an appropriate sum. Of course, the money does not have to be real, you can simply state that the buyer paid in cash, which means you only get to pay taxes for the transfer to fall through. The transfer does not also need to be real; you can strike a deal where you get to drive the car while it's under your "buyer's" name. As mentioned in previous chapters, cars and land are the most pursued assets in cases of debt default, and having no car registered in your name is a sure way to get annoying creditors off your backside.

If the car is leased or has finance and you don't have title to it, you cannot sell it. However, you can attempt to hide it so it cannot be repossessed. Repo teams cannot enter private property (garages), though they can go onto your drives. If your car is fitted with a GPS tracking device, find it and remove it. This is not illegal, it just breaches your loan conditions, which you are about to breach anyway. This will prevent the lease company from remotely disabling your vehicle and finding it.

3. Take More "Loans" - get a friendly creditor, ideally a good friend, ask them to give you a large, fake loan that matures in a few weeks, and attach your car or other valuable property as security. When the inevitable default happens, make an act of them officially taking ownership of the attached assets.

4. Transfer all your other assets to a friend, spouse, or family. Including investments, bank accounts, jewelry, furniture, cash. If you transfer them to your spouse then ensure that you live in a state where the property is not a shared asset (where you would continue to have a 50% interest).

5. Consider changing your employment if you believe

creditors may be able to trace where you work and garnish your wages.

Step 2 - Negotiating Settlements

Admittedly, it is not a given that your debt cleansing attempts will extinguish all your debt obligations. In some cases, the creditors may outsmart you, either in court or by gaining other forms of leverage over you. As a result, you would have to sit with them and figure out a way forward. But unlike in normal circumstances, you should approach these talks with assertiveness and make it clear to the lender that you know your rights and will defend yourself with everything.

The first thing to keep in mind when negotiating with lenders is to avoid debt settlement organizations and most nonprofit debt counseling agencies. Both of these types of institutions are known to play both sides during a settlement with the aim of getting higher cuts. If you do need advanced assistance in your endeavor, contact a trusted debt attorney.

When you get to the table, be clear from the start that you cannot afford to repay the debt, and explain the reasons. If you want your creditors to understand your situation and reconsider their stand, you need to appeal to their empathetic side. Afterward, suggest a "solution" where you commit to repay a part of the debt over an extended period of time. Make it clear that the alternative to this is the lender going to great lengths (and expenses) to recoup their money which, considering your presently low liquidity, will probably lead to even bigger losses for them. Creditors are generally more willing to renegotiate the payment terms or reduce the debt when all the other possible solutions seem expensive and time-consuming.

Step 3 - Slow or Stop the wheels of the "Process"

Your overall aim in this process is to make it so drawn out that your creditors repeatedly sell your debts at ever bigger discounts, giving you the chance to settle at pennies on the dollar, or even for them to be unenforceable at all. It is vital you keep all correspondence and call logs.

- Whenever a debt collection agency (CA) makes the first contact then challenge the validity of the debt as a matter of course. See chapter 3.
- Encourage the CA to breach the FDCPA by writing to them to stop all contact. Record any calls (ensuring that you inform them of this, as previously discussed).
- Ask for copies of all the loan documentation - if they cannot provide this they will probably not be able to enforce the debt in the courts. The plaintiff must supply a credit or loan agreement signed by you.
- Ask for proof of what you owe. Demand documentation that starts with the opening of your account and ends with the last activity on the account. The goal is they must account for every dollar they claim you owe.
- Has there been any interest or other charges added, and are the interest and the other charges added legally?
- When you receive papers use your own documentation to look for errors in the borrower or lender's details, including the account numbers, names, addresses, legal entities, and the amounts borrowed and owed. Any discrepancies can be exploited to ensure that judgment goes your way.

- At this point, you should engage a competent consumer debt attorney.
- See if you can counter sue for breaches of the FDCPA or FCRA or other consumer protection legislation.

FDCPA BREACHES TO LOOK OUT FOR:

It's against the law for a collector to sue you or threaten to sue you on a time-barred debt. File a complaint with the FTC and your state Attorney General, and consider talking to an attorney about bringing your own private action against the collector for violating the FDCPA.

- They are not allowed to contact you before 8 AM or after 9 PM unless you agree to it.
- They are not allowed to contact you at work if you have informed them, in writing or orally, that you are not allowed to get calls there.
- You are allowed to request the Collections Agency to stop contacting you via phone, and they will be required to continue only via written communication.
- They are not allowed to share the details of the account with anyone except the debtor.
- Contacting a consumer known to be represented by an attorney. Therefore ensure that all CA are notified if you engage an attorney. Your attorney should take care of this for you.
- Communication with third parties: revealing or discussing the nature of debts with third parties (other than the consumer's spouse or attorney).

Step 4 - Your Lenders Go To Court

It is always a possibility that you will get sued when you default on a loan. If you decide to 'cleanse' yourself of your debt obligations. However, that shouldn't worry you, according to Newbery. He shares an example of how one creditor, who he owed $5.8 million, battled him all the way to the Missouri Court of Appeals and guess who won? You are right.

And what made Newberry win the case was not that the lenders were wrong, or that he didn't owe the alleged debt. No, he only had to spot a few bits of shoddy legal work by his lender's attorneys in the court documents then use them as a get out of jail card. This is very easy to do as most creditors use pretty much the same attorneys who act as 'foreclosure mills' and the sheer amount of work these attorneys handle means that frequently, they will fail to include key documents in their submissions, including inaccurate details, or incomplete pages. If you are able to detect these inconsistencies and attract the court's attention to them, you will increase your leverage such that even if the court may eventually ask you to pay the debt, the costs of the continued litigation occasioned by your objections will be high enough for the lender to consider settling for a lower repayment.

The CA or Creditor (now the plaintiff in legalese) must have a copy of the Complaint delivered to you, so you will know about the lawsuit.

In the Complaint, (the) Plaintiff makes statements about you and about debts that Plaintiff believes you owe. The Plaintiff saying things about you in the complaint does not make them true. An Answer is your chance to tell the court which of Plaintiff's statements are true and should be admitted, which are not true and should be denied, and which statements you do not know or understand, or cannot remember if it is true (should be denied for lack of information).

You will also get a summons. This is NOT a notice of a court hearing date. It gives instructions about how to respond to the complaint. It tells you:

- You have a right to disagree with the Complaint in writing.
- How long you have to answer the Complaint. You have 20 days from the date the Complaint is handed to you or someone in your home, NOT 20 days from the date stamped on the Summons and Complaint.
- Where to deliver your answer.

Step 5 - They obtain judgment: How to Stop a Wage or Non-Wage Garnishment

Having your wages or bank account garnished can seriously affect your life and make it harder for you to meet your living costs and other expenses. Not being able to pay is not a defense. However, just because a court has ordered the garnishment of your wages doesn't mean your situation is completely hopeless. Although it has to be said it is preferable to stop the process before it gets to this point. However, there are a few options that you can take advantage of to stop the garnishment. Obviously, one of the surest ways to prevent your wages from being garnished is to simply pay back all the money that you owe to your creditors. However, if you don't have the money to do so, you will need to employ other strategies to stop the garnishment. Let us now look at some of the ways in which you can do so.

- Challenge the Garnishment

If you have reason to believe that the ruling to garnish

your wages is unfair or will significantly threaten your personal finances, you should carefully examine all the documents and look for errors in the named persons, addresses, or against other original documents. You should also not reveal your employer voluntarily and should aim to conceal this to prevent creditors from hounding them for personal information.

- Negotiate with Your Creditor

Contact your lenders and convince them to agree to your payment plan. Take a good look at your budget and decide on the amount that you can realistically pay. Once you have figured out what works for you, get in touch with your creditors and get them to agree with this repayment plan. It is important to note, however, that once a creditor has successfully won a garnishment claim, they do not need to agree with your payment plan or even pursue it. So, the success of this approach is highly dependent on your ability to make a good case and convince your creditors that you will honor your promise should they agree to it.

- File a Claim of Exemption

Depending on your personal and financial situation, you may be able to stop a wage garnishment or reduce the amount by filing a claim of exemption. Some states provide an exemption to debtors who are household heads and have people who depend on them, for instance, elderly parents or young kids. We provided a discussion of exempt income in chapter 2.

Provide a Declaration of Exempt Income and Assets. This declaration is a sworn statement that lets your creditors know you have income and/or assets the law says they may not take from you. If you think your income is protected or exempt from garnishment, you must still respond, but you should also consult a lawyer.

People with very few assets and small incomes may be "judgment-proof," because legal protections exempt them from collection. But that does not mean you can ignore a judgment. It takes work to determine that your wages and belongings are protected from seizure by state and federal exemptions. You must take action to deter wrongful collection attempts on your exempt property before they happen.

THE DEBT CLEANSE APPROACH TO MORTGAGES

I am going to level with you here. In my opinion, this is not a strategy that you should attempt if you have built up any significant equity *(the difference between what it is worth now and what you bought it for)* in your house. This is because you put that at risk, and that actually makes your negotiating position weaker *(your lender can look up a valuation)*. In that instance reconsider the use of debt consolidation as a tool. The second reason is that the pressure of potential eviction will put you, your family, and relationship under an immense amount of pressure.

However, if you feel you have no other choices left open to you, here is what you must do. You could also use this to try and get a better deal, backing off at the last moment if you don't succeed and then bringing your account up to date, however that will have destroyed your credit rating.

If you have failed to negotiate any modification to the terms of your mortgage, which is quite likely as many mortgage companies will not consider any modification until you are 60 days delinquent, then be assured there is still a process. This procedure must legally be followed by lenders if they want to foreclose and evict you from your property.

Once you stop making mortgage payments, you should also stop paying property taxes as these will be the responsibility of your creditor if they repossess the property *(thus reducing the value of the property to them)*. Newbery also recommends ceasing to pay any HELOC or second loan.

Next, request a mortgage modification packet from your lender. simply say that your circumstances have changed and you cannot pay. Fill in the documents and return them to your lender. Consider the payments you can afford versus the current payment and also how much, if any equity, you have in the house. Also, consider the rates that customers in good standing are paying.

The mortgage company will generally process and consider your request before proceeding with the foreclosure process. Ensure that you have done this before you are 120 days delinquent.

The process can take a number of months because these companies are bureaucratic and move slowly. In case you are asked to provide any information or clarification, you should respond, but only after the maximum time has elapsed. If they give you 30 days to respond, then take 26 days. Always use registered communications and keep copies.

When you request a mortgage modification, you should expect calls from your lender. You should resist any temptation to elaborate or make a payment; this is just part of the process, they are obliged to let you make an application.

If your application is successful and *reasonable,* then happy days. If you are denied or not happy with it, then appeal the decision - you will have 14 days to do this. The loan service company has 30 days to respond. They will most likely decline your application.

At this point, make an offer (in writing and recorded delivery) to settle your delinquency. Offer 3 months of whatever you are proposing as your new mortgage payment, and demand that any charges or back payments are written off. Also, demand that the principal be reduced to 95% of the value of your home (if it is higher than the current valuation).

If your offer is rejected, then you will receive a demand letter (breach notice or letter of acceleration). This gives you 30 days to bring your payments up to date. You may also receive additional pre-foreclosure notices, depending on which state you live in. At this point, you should submit a Qualified Written Request (QWR). You can submit this at any time, between receipt of the demand letter and before the start of the foreclosure action. This little hand grenade will have your lender jumping through hoops. Again they are obliged to respond.

The QWR demands that they prove you owe what is alleged. It is much more detailed than the verification process used for unsecured lending. Some companies will put the foreclosure process on hold while they respond. In any case, they have 5 business days to acknowledge your request and 30 days to respond in full. If you do not receive a response in time, then send a reminder. This forms part of your file that is useful if the case goes to litigation.

At this point, it is up to you and your attorney to identify and exploit discrepancies and deficiencies in the documentation and QWR of the mortgage company - things like robo signatures and missing assignments of titles. The purpose of this is to encourage the lender to sell your debt at a big discount, which you can then exploit to settle at a fraction of its original value.

In summary:

- A debt cleanse is a strategy that is designed to wear down the lender and make them incur high recovery expenses so that they stop chasing you or

at least delay the inevitable long enough to allow you to organize your finances.
- When embarking on a debt cleanse, always ensure that you seal off all loopholes by transferring ownership of your land and properties to a trust fund, selling off your car and transferring all your other assets to a third party such as your friend, spouse, or other family members.
- Be very clear with your creditors that you are not able to repay the debt.
- Slow down the process of negotiating a settlement until it is too untenable or unenforceable.

CHAPTER NINE: DEBT SPECIFIC INFORMATION

In this the penultimate chapter, I want to provide some information that you could find useful when dealing with different types of debt. I will highlight specific things that we haven't covered much, like how to deal with the IRS *(carefully, very carefully)*, student and medical debt, and payday loans for example.

Let's start with utilities as debts to utility companies are a common problem.

UTILITY DEBTS

Generally, consumer protections apply only to gas and electric services - however, propane or heating oil that is delivered is not regulated. Water is usually provided by a government provider which is far less regulated. There are no federal laws that specifically protect utility customers; those rights come under state laws.

Services may be provided by Investor-Owned Utilities (IOUs), government-owned entities (munis), or rural electric cooperatives (co-ops). Gas and electric service is typically regulated by Public Utility Commissions (PUCs).

The statute of limitations (SOL) could prevent a utility company, or CA, from suing you to collect. That time period is based on state law and will be the same as the statute of limitations for contract actions. Utility debts are still covered by the FDCPA and FCRA, so the same restriction and protections will apply to CA as for any other debt. However, remember these will not apply to utility companies collecting their own debts.

Probably the best way to deal with these debts if you don't want to get cut off is to request a payment plan. However, only agree to a payment plan you can afford as in some states, you may not get the same advance notice of termination if you fall behind on a payment plan.

Find out about budget billing or 'levelized' payments. Those plans allow you to pay a similar amount each month, adjusted periodically depending on your use. Generally, this keeps your bills roughly the same even in the coldest and hottest months.

About twenty or so states offer protection against service termination if you are ill or have a very low income. Many states offer protection to particular types of customers during the winter months. In those states, service can't be disconnected during certain months of the year or when the temperature falls below a certain level, or you may be allowed to pay a smaller amount to avoid cut-off.

There may also be specific protections available if someone living in your home has a serious illness that could be threatened by a shut-off, e.g. a young child, elderly, or disabled family member.

HOW TO NEGOTIATE BACK TAXES WITH IRS

When considering your position with the IRS, it is wise to remember that Al Capone was only brought down by failing to pay his taxes and the government has almost unlimited powers to make you pay up. More bankruptcies are brought by the IRS than any financial institution.

In case you have been falling behind on your tax payments, it is absolutely crucial that you take proactive steps to address the issue and negotiate a payment plan that works for you with the Internal Revenue Service (IRS). Here are some of the steps you can take if you are facing a tough time and are unable to pay your taxes on time:

- Ensure You File Your Tax Returns

Even if you owe the IRS a substantial amount of money that you are unable to pay all at once, it is still a good idea to file your tax returns. Most people often make the mistake of failing to file their tax returns since they don't have the money to pay their taxes that are due. This, however, is not a good approach to take since it results in them paying much more in penalties than they would otherwise do if they had filed their returns.

While the IRS may not immediately start charging penalties in case you delay in tax payment, eventually they will do so. This might take weeks or even months but ultimately, it is going to happen. While their collection efforts may seem very benign at first, sooner or later, they are going to get more aggressive and start seeking wage levies from your employer. This can put you in a very strenuous financial position since a huge chunk of your wages will be going directly to the IRS.

In order to protect yourself, therefore, you need to act as

soon as you receive your first back-tax notice and take advantage of the various options that are available to you. These include:

1. Requesting the IRS to temporarily delay collection on your taxes until you are in a better financial position and able to pay your taxes
2. Negotiate an installment agreement so that you are allowed to pay your outstanding taxes over a given period of time
3. Seek a compromise that allows you to make a lump-sum payment that is less than what you owe.

In most cases, the IRS will be willing to work with any of these options. However, whether they opt for an installment agreement or a lump sum, payment typically depends on your financial situation. In order to decide which option is best for you, they might request you to fill out forms to ascertain your sources of income, debts, and liabilities. If they have reason to believe that you are able to fulfill your tax obligations, they will probably not compromise much.

- Opt for an Installment Agreement

Choosing a payment plan that works for you is probably the best option since it will cost you the least, and will likely be least detrimental for you. Submitting a request to the IRS for an installment agreement is likely to yield the best results if:

i) You assure the IRS that you will pay off your outstanding debt within six years *(preferably within three years)*

ii) The monthly installments that you propose to pay are

equal to or higher than what the IRS would receive from a settlement agreement that it initiates.

You should keep in mind that once an agreed-upon payment plan has been made, interest and penalties will continue to accrue until the outstanding back-tax balance is fully settled.

- Do not Default on Payments

Once you have reached an agreement with the IRS, you should try as much as possible to make payments on time. At this point, you should prioritize this debt over any of the others. Failure to comply with the terms of the arrangement may result in the IRS putting a lien on your property or claiming your bank accounts. If *(for whatever reason)* you are unable to make payment as required, contact the IRS and try to seek a temporary delay on collection so that you can buy yourself more time to get your finances in order.

PAYDAY LOANS

Payday loans are some of the most common and detrimental consumer debts that working people usually incur. These loans are toxic and should be avoided at all costs. While these loans provide you with an easy line of credit *(particularly if you don't have collateral to help you get secured loans)*, they will keep you trapped in a vicious cycle of debt. Knowing how to handle these types of loans is therefore crucial if you are serious about getting out of debt a lot faster.

WHAT ARE PAYDAY LOANS AND HOW DO THEY WORK?

A payday loan is essentially a short-term loan *(usually $100 - $1500)*, that enables you to cover your bills and expenses until your next paycheck arrives. Depending on the state where you live, you may be able to secure a payday loan online or through a physical branch that provides these types of loans. Different states have various laws that govern payday lending. These laws put caps on the amount of money you can borrow and how much interest and fees a lender can charge on the loan. Some states even prohibit payday loans entirely.

In case you apply for a payday loan and your request gets approved, you may receive the money in form of a check, physical cash, or direct bank deposit. You will then be required to pay back the loan in full, in addition to the finance charge by the due date, usually about 14 days.

Despite the high costs of these loans, many people still take them on a regular basis. This is because they provide an easy line of credit, particularly to individuals who lack other financing options due to poor credit ratings or no income. Payday loans typically have very few qualification requirements and lenders usually don't check the credit score of borrowers when deciding whether to give them loans. In most cases, you only need to have identification, a bank account that is in relatively good standing, and a reliable paycheck in order to qualify for a payday loan.

Unlike other types of loans such as mortgages and car loans, payday loans are not secured by any personal asset or property. This essentially means your lender cannot seize or lay claim to your property in case you default on the repayment, or at least not without a court judgment. They can still send collectors to coerce you or even take you to court for any outstanding balances that you owe.

The biggest downside of payday loans is that they tend to accrue very high-interest rates. Depending on the state where you live, the interest rate of a payday loan can average over 400%. To put this into perspective, most personal loans usually charge interest of between 4%-35% while interest rates for credit cards usually range between 12%-30%. Since lenders of these loans often don't verify an individual's ability to pay back these loans, some borrowers often end up taking a very high APR and are unable to pay back what they owe.

As payday loans are usually for smaller amounts of less than $500 it isn't usually economic for the lender to take you to court, this is why they employ high-pressure collection tactics. This combined with the toxic rates of interest means that payday lenders will probably agree to some kind of payment plan, where the interest will be frozen or reduced and you settle outright or pay off over a short defined period.

ALTERNATIVES TO PAYDAY LENDERS

For a more reasonable alternative to payday lenders, search out your local credit union. Their interest rates will be much more reasonable, and they will be generally more pleasant to deal with. However they may be slower to deal with; so plan and act in advance to avoid payday lenders.

NEGOTIATING WITH YOUR LANDLORD/AGENT

Paying your monthly rent in full and on time is without a doubt your biggest obligation as a tenant. If you have fallen behind on your rent payments due to unforeseen circumstances or any other reason, it is critical that you communicate your situation to your landlord or agent. Failing to do so can put you in a breach of tenancy, for which your landlord can pursue legal action against you and put you at risk of eviction.

If you have rent arrears, but still wish to continue living

on the property, you need to take the necessary steps to negotiate a payment plan with your landlord to minimize the likelihood of eviction.

Before defaulting on your rent arrears you will probably be aware that many landlords will ask for references from previous tenancies, and this could prevent you from finding reasonable and legal housing. Here are some of the steps that you need to take if you have rent arrears:

- See whether you can claim some social security benefits to cover this.
- If you are unable to clear your outstanding rent arrears, but have some funds, then use the lessons in chapters 5 and 6 to negotiate with your landlord to settle the arrears for less than the full amount. If your problems can be described as a temporary difficulty and you otherwise have a good track record with your landlord, they may well be flexible. There is little alternative for them to recover the money, as it represents lost rental time - they cannot rent that time again, they may take what they can get. However, you will have to sell them the idea that the circumstances were beyond control and purely temporary but you don't have sufficient funds, and never will, to clear the arrears.

STUDENT DEBT

Student loan debt has become a hot political topic in the recent past and for a good reason. According to the Department of Education, the total U.S. student loan debt stands at over $1.6 trillion, which makes it the second-largest personal debt category, only behind mortgage debt. To put it in context, 45 million students own more debt cumulatively than the over 100 million car owners with auto loans.

If you were a college student, it is highly likely that you have loans used to pay for your education, considering that two-thirds of all college students do.

Private Loans vs Federal Loans: What's The Difference?

Student loans generally fall into two distinct categories; private and federal. The terms of issue and repayment are entirely dependent on which type of loan you take.

Private loans are typically provided by banks, credit unions, individual lenders, or even the institution itself, while federal loans (also known as federal student aid) are funded by the federal government. The difference between the two is as great as night and day. On one side, private loans are purely driven by a profit motive on the side of the lender instead of the academic needs of the borrower. Apart from being hard to qualify for (creditworthiness is the main consideration), they also have higher interest rates and more rigid repayment terms. Federal loans, on the other hand, have more open qualification procedures - as almost all university students qualify, carry lower interest rates, and have more flexible payment terms. With federal loans, there is also some very limited chance of debt forgiveness, either as a political move or after meeting certain eligibility requirements. However, they are not discharged by bankruptcy.

If you're wondering - yes, it is possible to take multiple loans as long as you qualify for all of them. In case you choose to go this route, consider consolidating all the debt together so you only have to make a single payment per month instead of having multiple due dates. Notably, it is easier to consolidate federal loans than private ones, as the former is envisaged in the Federal Direct Consolidation Loan program while private loans are governed by the agreed terms.

Student Loan Restructuring and Debt "Haircuts"

Notably, if you are not able to make a payment on your federal loan 270 days after your last one, you will be considered to have defaulted while private loans enter default state after 120 days of missed payments. It is at these stages that settlement talks can commence. However, agreeing to a settlement on a federal loan is quite hard as the Department of Education has far-reaching debt-collection powers and is especially fond of wage and tax refund garnishment.

On the other hand, private loan holders are generally more willing to negotiate settlements as they have limited debt collection ability.

How Much Can You Save in A Debt Haircut?

For private student loan debt, how much you can save from a settlement depends on who owns your debt. Some lenders may only agree to take 80% or more of the loaned amount while others may accept even 50%, depending on your circumstances. Use the negotiating tactics in chapters six and seven to get the best deal.

Federal loans are relatively more rigid in that the options are limited and the potential savings aren't much irrespective of your situation. Generally, the Department of Education will give you the following 3 choices when you approach them with a settlement proposal:

- Pay full principal with 100% waiver on collection costs
- 50% waiver on the accrued interest
- 10% waiver of both the principal and interest

Alternative settlement methods on federal loans are rare, as they require approval from the Department, which can take quite a while.

How to Save Money on Student Debt

The most common way of saving money on student debt is to pay it all within a short time frame. For instance, if you have a $30,000 loan on 2.84% and a 10-year repayment plan, you will pay a total of $4,384.11 in interest if you spread the payments over the stipulated term. However, if you pay it all in one year, your interest paid will only be $503.88, which means you save about $3,880. Of course, you don't have to overburden yourself by paying all the debt in a year, you could give it 2-3 years and the savings would still be considerable.

You will save a lot more on interest if you finish repaying your loan in one or two years.

VEHICLE FINANCE

While in the past people had the time to save and pay for their cars in cash, today's ever-changing social-economic reality means that many prospective car owners choose to take out loans to get their cars.

Car loans work pretty much the same way as other secured loans. Basically, your lender will provide you with the funds to buy the car you want whereas you undertake to pay back the full amount, with interest, in the form of monthly payments. If you fail to clear the loan, the lender will be entitled to repossess the car (they don't have to give you specific notice of this) and resell it in order to recover their investment.

What Happens When You Can't Pay Your Car Loan?

If you find yourself in a position where you can't pay off your auto loan, you can either sit pretty and wait for the lender to repossess it (and mess your credit score in the process), or sell the car and use the proceeds to pay the remaining debt. If, however, you still want to keep the car, you can contact the lender and work out a repayment plan that will allow you to do so while reducing your monthly debt burden. As it is, lenders only pursue vehicle repossession as a measure of last resort because, unlike other types of assets, the value of cars depreciates over time, which means the lender is unlikely to recover their money even if they auction the repossessed car.

When negotiating a new payment plan, talks will more likely be focused on the following areas:

- Altering the interest rate - The options here are; either you ask your lender to reduce your monthly interest rates in exchange for a longer repayment term *(and higher cumulative interest)* or refinance the loan with another low-interest loan. Be careful while at it though, as an extended payment term may significantly increase the total debt even when the monthly interest is low.
- Reduction of the overall debt - This is often the hardest thing to convince an auto lender to do, as it means they suffer a loss. Nonetheless, if you can prove to them that you are under severe financial duress and cannot afford to complete the repayment and that they may not be able to recover the full loan amount even when they repossess the car, you may have a chance. The con is that they may blacklist you for that, making it harder for you to access loans in the future.
- Extension of the payment term - If you present a sensible argument, the lender may agree to extend your repayment period, which means you will have more time to reorganize your finances and pay the loan. However, you may be forced to pay a "penalty", either in the form of additional interest, or a flat fee.

MEDICAL DEBTS

Like credit card and other unsecured debt, you may have the option of settling the medical debt for less than what is owed. Settling a medical debt is the same as settling any other type of debt. You should contact the doctor, hospital, or collection agency to begin negotiations. Often, they will agree to accept a reduced amount.

Our advice is that you start the settlement process as early as possible before your healthcare provider gives the debt over to a collection company. In cases of medical debt, a collection agency has significantly less motivation to settle than a doctor or hospital would.

Offering a reduced lump sum payment is the most effective approach. The secret lies in getting enough money to make a compelling offer. Second, making small payments over time is another method - most health care providers will have offered you this alternative already, but you may be able to get a better deal if you can demonstrate financial hardship. Ensure that the creditor agrees, in writing, to this plan.

If you have a verifiable hardship, like a disability that prevents you from working, you may be able to seek medical bill forgiveness. In this case, petition the provider to forgive the debt entirely. Your provider will want to see proof, in the form of tax returns and written documentation, that you have no means to pay your medical bills. You can also apply to non-profit organizations like the PAN Foundation and CancerCare for help with your medical bills.

Unpaid medical bills will impact your credit score. Usually, doctors and hospitals don't report debts to credit bureaus but pass their unpaid bills over to a debt collection agency and it is the CA that reports them.

In summary, here are the key points to note from this chapter:

- If you have fallen behind on your taxes, the best way to approach the situation is to take proactive steps to negotiate with the IRS for: a temporary delay of payment, an agreement to pay in installments or a lump sum payment that is less than you owe.
- Always file your tax returns with the IRS even if you are unable to pay taxes since this gives you a better chance when negotiating a settlement.
- Payday loans are generally very expensive and should be avoided. Seek out credit unions instead for personal loans since these institutions generally offer better interest rates and terms.
- If you are struggling with rent arrears, try to negotiate with your landlord for an extension to allow you to get your cards in order and check if you may qualify for social security benefits which may help you cover some of the costs.
- If you have a car loan, you may choose an extension of the payment term, a reduction of the overall debt or alteration of the interest rate, just to ensure the car isn't repossessed by your creditor.
- The most appropriate method of saving money on student debt is to pay it all within a short time frame.

CHAPTER TEN: THE NUCLEAR SOLUTION TO DEBT - HOW TO BLOW UP YOUR DEBT

In Chapter Two, we looked at how filing for bankruptcy can be used as a strategy to get out of debt. In this chapter, we are going to delve more into what that means, including the definitions, consequences, and the options that are available to you.

CHAPTER 13 BANKRUPTCY

A Chapter 13 bankruptcy is also commonly referred to as a *'wage earner's plan'.* This essentially enables you to create a plan to pay off part or all of your debts if you still have a regular income. Under this plan, you *(the debtor)* are expected to come up with a payment proposal to make regular installments to your creditors over a period of three to five years. If your current monthly income is less than the applicable state median, then the payment plan will be for three years unless a court approves a longer-term. On the other hand, if your current monthly income is greater than the applicable state median then the payment plan must be for five years. Under no circumstance will the payment plan exceed five years.

During this period, your creditors and/or debt collectors are legally barred from starting or continuing with the collection.

Advantages of Chapter 13 Bankruptcy

If you are struggling with debt payments, there are a number of advantages that you can derive from Chapter 13. These include:

- Protecting Your Home against Foreclosure

One of the main benefits of Chapter 13 is that it offers you the opportunity to save your home from foreclosure. By filing bankruptcy under this chapter, you can halt foreclosure proceedings. However, you will still be required to make all mortgage payments on time.

- Reschedule Secured Debts

Filing for Chapter 13 bankruptcy also allows you to reschedule your secured debts (with the exception of mortgage payments) thus extending their term over the duration of the Chapter 13 plan. This can help to reduce minimum payments so that you are able to pay your secured debts more comfortably.

- Functions in a Similar Way to Loan Consolidation

If you are unable to secure a consolidated loan to pay off your outstanding debts, Chapter 13 makes a provision that is designed to accomplish more or less the same thing. When you file for bankruptcy under Chapter 13, you will be required to make payments to a Chapter 13 trustee who then distributes the money to your creditors.

Chapter 13 Bankruptcy Process

While the procedure for a Chapter 13 bankruptcy is fairly simple, it is important to understand what you are getting into. Remember, you will be required to make payments to a trustee for the next three or five years. To initiate the bankruptcy, you will need to file a lengthy set of bankruptcy forms and attend a minimum of two meetings. Once the case is finalized you will receive a discharge on some of your debts.

Let us now go over the entire process and what you can expect:

- Complete a Credit Counseling Course

Within six months prior to filing for Chapter 13 bankruptcy, you must take a credit counseling course from an agency that has been approved by the U.S Trustees office. You can find the list of approved agencies on the U.S Trustees website.

- Prepare Your Petition

You will be required to complete a batch of forms, which include the bankruptcy petition, schedules, and other forms. You will need to disclose your assets, debts, income, and any property transfers that you may have conducted. Furthermore, you must draft and submit a Chapter 13 repayment plan.

- File the Bankruptcy Petition, Proposed Plan and Tax Information

You will be expected to file your bankruptcy petition along with your payment plan in addition to your most recent tax returns.

- Court Appoints a Bankruptcy Trustee to Administer Your Case

Once you have tabled your bankruptcy petition, the court will appoint a trustee whose role is to review your plan and ensure that it complies with the law. Your trustee is also charged with collecting payments and distributing them to your creditors as well as monitoring your monthly income and expenses.

- The Automatic Stay Takes Effect

Upon filing your papers, the bankruptcy automatic stay goes into effect. This prohibits your creditors from proceeding with the collection

- You Make Your First Chapter 13 Plan Payment

You are required to start making payments about one month after you file your papers even when your plan is pending confirmation by the court.

- Attend Meetings with Creditors

Your trustee will preside over meetings between you and your creditors in a room other than a courtroom. They will interrogate you about your papers and finances. Your creditors are also allowed to ask questions and can object to your payment plan if they feel the need to do so.

- Attend the Confirmation Hearing

Either you or your attorney will be expected to attend a confirmation hearing in court, during which the court will address any objections that have been raised by your creditors or trustee. If there are no pertinent issues, then the court will promptly confirm your plan

- Comply with the Payment Plan and make Payments

Once your plan has been confirmed by the court, you will be required to abide by the payment plan and make payments as agreed. You may also be required to present documents such as your income and expenses statement

- Complete a Personal Financial Management Class

As part of the Chapter 13 plan, you will be required to complete a debtor education class before the end of your bankruptcy case.

- Court Grants You a Discharge and Closes Your Case

Once the repayment period elapses, the court will grant you a discharge, which essentially wipes out any remaining balance of your debt. In some cases, the court may set a discharge hearing which you are expected to physically attend or it may opt to mail you the notice of discharge instead.

CHAPTER 7 LIQUIDATION OF ASSETS

Unlike Chapter 13 bankruptcy, Chapter 7 does not involve filing a payment plan. Instead, this bankruptcy code provides that a trustee gathers and sells a debtor's non-exempt assets and uses the proceeds to pay creditors. It is worth noting that some of a debtor's assets may be subject to liens, which means they are owned by other creditors. Chapter 7 bankruptcy may allow a debtor to keep some of their exempt assets property but the trustee will liquidate all their remaining assets. You should be very cautious when filing a Chapter 7 bankruptcy since this might result in you losing your property and possessions.

Under this statute, unsecured debts are separated into different categories and paid off in order of priority. Secured debts on the other hand are backed by a collateral to minimize the risk associated with lending. Unsecured debts such as child support payments, tax debts, and personal injury claims are paid off first, followed by secured debts such as mortgages and car loans.

Chapter 7 Bankruptcy Process

Here are some of the steps that you can expect to go through when filing for a Chapter 7 bankruptcy:

- Complete a Credit Counseling Course

You are expected to undergo credit counseling within six months prior to filing for Chapter 7 bankruptcy. In the event that there is no approved agency in your state, you may be allowed to forgo this step. Exceptions may also be made depending on your personal circumstances.

- File the Bankruptcy Petition

Once you have completed the credit counseling course, you will be required to complete a batch of forms and file a petition with the court. Some of the personal information that you are expected to provide include, your assets, expenses, income, and details of your creditors.

- Automatic Stay Takes Effect

After you have tabled your bankruptcy petition, an automatic stay will take effect, and this prevents your debt collectors and creditors from proceeding with the collection. The stay will also halt any wage garnishments that are ongoing.

- Appointment of a Trustee

The court will appoint a trustee who is charged with the task of overseeing the bankruptcy process. The trustee will schedule and preside over meetings between you and your creditors out of court, and conduct a review of your assets to determine which ones can be liquidated to pay off your creditors.

- Attend Meetings with Creditors

You will be required to attend meetings with your creditors where you will be interrogated about your finances. Your creditors will also get a chance to ask you questions and verify the validity of your petition.

- Debt Repayment

Your assigned trustee will review your personal assets and finances to decide which properties can be liquidated for repayment of debts. Exempt property and any other properties that you need in order to maintain a basic standard of living will be left in your possession.

- Discharge of Remaining Debt

Chapter 7 bankruptcy allows for debt discharges which

release you from any personal liability for payment. Once a debt balance is discharged, your creditors will no longer be able to seek restitution from you. However, there are certain debts that are exempted from discharge. These include child support, alimony payments, federal student loan, and some government taxes.

CONSEQUENCES OF BANKRUPTCY

Filing for bankruptcy is a serious decision that should never be taken lightly since it comes with ramifications. If you are thinking about blowing up your debt by claiming bankruptcy, it is important to understand the consequences that such a decision will have.

One of the main consequences of filing for bankruptcy is the loss of property. Regardless of whether you opt for a Chapter 7 or Chapter 13 bankruptcy, you may be required to give up some of your property for liquidation in order to pay back your creditors. Under certain circumstances, filing for bankruptcy can lead to the loss of your property (home), car, jewelry, antiques, and other valuables.

Bankruptcy can also have adverse financial implications for people close to you. For instance, if you cosign for a car loan with your spouse, that is a joint asset and they may be held liable for some of that debt in case you file for bankruptcy.

In addition to this, filing for bankruptcy can significantly affect your credit. Bankruptcies are generally considered as negative information on your credit report and may affect how future lenders view you. Having a bankruptcy on your credit report can make lenders very reluctant to give you loans, and in case you find a lender who is willing to lend you money, they are likely to charge very exorbitant interest rates and give you unfavorable terms.

Bankruptcy can stay on your credit reports for up to 10 years, showing up even after your debts are discharged and the bankruptcy is completed.

SHOULD YOU FILE FOR CHAPTER 7 OR CHAPTER 13 BANKRUPTCY?

In most cases, filing for Chapter 7 is usually a better option than Chapter 13. The process for Chapter 7 usually takes less time and it typically allows you to retain possession of most of your property. However, sometimes you may not be eligible for a Chapter 7 bankruptcy, and even if you are, it may not meet your needs. Nevertheless, there are a number of reasons why filing for Chapter 7 may be the best option for you. These include:

- It is Relatively Quick

The process of filing for a Chapter 7 bankruptcy takes between three to six months to complete.

- No Payment Plan Required

Unlike a Chapter 13 bankruptcy which requires you to make a three or five-year payment plan to pay off your debts, Chapter 7 bankruptcy makes no such provision.

- Most of Your Debts get Discharged

Filing a Chapter 7 bankruptcy can free you of all your debts with only a few exceptions. Some of the debts that are not exempted from this type of bankruptcy include student loans, alimony payments, child support, and government taxes.

- You can Protect Your Property

While there is a possibility that you may lose your property when you file for Chapter 7 bankruptcy, in most cases, you will be able to keep everything you own. Filing for a Chapter 7 bankruptcy allows you to keep your necessities, and in case you don't own a lot of luxury goods, chances are that all your property will be exempted from repossession or liquidation.

When Is Chapter 7 Bankruptcy the Best Option For You?

Filing for Chapter 7 bankruptcy would be the most ideal option for you if:

- You don't own a lot of property
- Only have personal loans, credit card debt, and medical bills *(these will automatically be wiped out)*
- Your family median income does not exceed the state median for a family of your size

Before filing for Chapter 7, you will be required to take a test to determine whether your income makes you eligible for this chapter. If your income is less than the state median for a family of your size, you will automatically qualify for this bankruptcy. However, if after deducting all your allowances and expenses you still have enough money left over to make payments to your creditors, then you will not be eligible for Chapter 7.

When Is Chapter 13 Bankruptcy the Best Option for You?

There are some instances, Chapter 7 bankruptcy may not be very ideal for you. For example, if you have debts that are not dischargeable such as federal student loans, income tax debt, and alimony payments, then Chapter 7 really won't be of much help to you. If your income is high you are also unlikely to qualify for this bankruptcy. Furthermore, if you are likely to lose substantial equity on your home if you file for Chapter 7, then this may not be the best option for you. In such circumstances, filing for Chapter 13 would be a much more desirable and beneficial alternative for you. However, the drawback of filing for Chapter 13 is that you will be required to pay all your disposable income (the money you are left with after expenses) to your creditors for three or five years. You may still be able to keep your home or car after filing for Chapter 13, but in order to do so, you will need to pay the arrears that you owe over the life of the bankruptcy.

Despite the challenges that Chapter 13 bankruptcy may present, it is still the best option to go with if you still receive a regular income which you can put into the payment plan to pay your creditors, and you may ultimately protect your home from foreclosure.

FILING MULTIPLE BANKRUPTCIES

There are limitations to being able to file multiple bankruptcies, but there are times when this may be advisable. You'll have to wait eight years after the filing date of the first Chapter 7 case before being able to file a second case. Before you'll be entitled to receive a second Chapter 13 discharge two years must elapse between filing dates.

When filing under different chapters the order matters. If the court granted your first discharge under Chapter 13 bankruptcy, you'd need to wait six years (from the Chapter 13 bankruptcy filing date) before filing for a Chapter 7 discharge. However, if you paid at least 70% of the claims in the Chapter 13 case you won't have to wait that long. If the court granted your first discharge under Chapter 7, you'll have to wait four years from the Chapter 7 filing date before filing a Chapter 13 case.

When a Second Filing Might be Beneficial Even Without a Discharge

Sometimes you don't need a discharge, you just need time to pay off a debt. For example, you owe federal taxes that you couldn't discharge in bankruptcy and you were unable to work out a reasonable payment plan. Instead of having your wages garnished, you could file for Chapter 13 bankruptcy and elongate the payments into a five-year Chapter 13 bankruptcy plan.

A similar approach is to file a Chapter 13 case immediately after receiving a Chapter 7 discharge (a procedure informally referred to as a Chapter 20 bankruptcy). Again, a common reason to do so is to secure additional time to pay off nondischargeable debts, such as domestic support obligation arrears.

Some courts don't allow the process, and it can be difficult to qualify for a Chapter 7 bankruptcy and then show that you have the available income to pay into a Chapter 13 plan.

In all cases, it is a good idea to consult with a specialist bankruptcy attorney before proceeding.

In summary, here are the key takeaways to remember from this chapter:

- Bankruptcy is a final solution to a chronic debt problem and can help you to reset your finances without getting stuck in a cycle of debt repayment indefinitely.
- There are two main types of bankruptcy, namely Chapter 7 and Chapter 13 which may be uniquely suited to you depending on your situation.
- Chapter 7 bankruptcy involves liquidation of non-exempt assets whose proceeds are then used to pay off your creditors.

- Chapter 13 bankruptcy involves a payment plan where all of your disposable income is used to pay off your creditors over a period of three or five years.
- In both types of bankruptcy, you will be eligible for a discharge of some debts with a few exceptions such as income tax, student loans, alimony payments, and child support which are non-dischargeable.

FINAL WORDS

So as we reach the conclusion of this book, I sincerely believe that you will be able to use the solutions that we have outlined to help you to crush your debts. If you have been wrestling with runaway debt that is eating into your income month after month, year after year, it is easy to feel despondent and hopeless about your financial situation. Being hounded and threatened by creditors and debt collectors can be a very frustrating and depressing situation. Now you are armed with the knowledge to begin planning your way forward to taking the right steps to navigate your debt, and ultimately pull yourself out of the debt trap.

We have seen what it means to have unsustainable debt and how to tell if your debt is ballooning out of control. Knowing how to identify runaway debt is absolutely crucial to reining in your debt since unfettered borrowing can lead to a very high debt-to-income ratio, which can negatively affect not only your ability to pay your outstanding debts but also diminish your creditworthiness.

We have looked at the steps and processes that your creditors may go through to try and get you to pay up, right up to enforcement judgments that they may pursue to recover their money. However, we have also examined all the various legal provisions that protect your rights and how you can use these to fight debt collectors. We have also set out six different approaches for managing your debts:

- Pay the debts using debt snowball or debt avalanche methods
- Consolidate the debts to get lower payments using a debt consolidation loan
- Use a debt management plan to pay off loans over 3 to 5 years
- Negotiate and settle (or reduce the cost of) the debt
- Repudiate the debt
- Declare bankruptcy

As we discussed many of these can be used in a mix and match way to provide your total strategy.

We showed in detail how you can use our 3-step strategy for negotiating with creditors in order to get the best outcome. The method that we have discussed in this book has been tried and tested and shown to yield spectacular results. So, if you are still in a position to negotiate a settlement with your creditors, this strategy will help you to seal the best deal and get the results. We have covered leverage and recourse that may be available to your creditors when it comes to secure and unsecured debts, so keeping these in mind should help you avoid common mistakes when negotiating with your creditors and also give you some leverage.

Finally, we have looked at the nuclear option for crushing debt, namely, bankruptcy. We have seen the two common types of bankruptcy and their distinctive characteristics as well as made a case for each of these. Depending on your

FINAL WORDS

debt situation, you may be eligible for either or both of these. However, you need to be careful when considering bankruptcy because, as we have seen, neither is without its consequences. You should therefore be very aware of the implications of each before deciding whether bankruptcy is the best option for you.

If anything, the position that you are in is simply a wake-up call for you that provides you with the opportunity to re-evaluate your financial habits *(borrowing and spending)* so that you can emerge on the other side debt free and reset your financial life. By applying the wisdom outlined in this book, you will be able to crush your debt and improve your financial situation for the foreseeable future. So don't procrastinate any longer. Take the bull by its horns today and begin to eliminate your grinding debt for good.

I have created a number of super useful resources that you can access by subscribing for a free personal finance toolkit including templates for many common letters and a debt repayment calculator (work out when your debt will be repaid for different interest rates, principals and repayments). Go to www.PersonalFinanceWizard.com.

AUTHOR'S NOTE

Thank you for reading my book. I very much hope you enjoyed it and found it informative. You may be aware that Amazon reviews are critical for independent authors; without these, my work will never be seen, that is just the way the system works. I would like to ask you to spend two minutes to leave a review for me, and be assured I personally read all my reviews. Your review will have a massive social influence on who will read my book as most people check the reviews. If you have never left a review before, just give one or two points around your main impressions and what you enjoyed. **Thanks, please go to the LINK below or scan QR code:**

https://www.amazon.com/review/create-review?ie=UTF8&channel=glance-detail&asin=B08LN76V6S

REFERENCES

A 6-Step Guide to Paying Off Your Debt. (n.d.). The Balance. Retrieved October 2, 2020, from https://www.thebalance.com/how-to-set-up-a-debt-payment-plan-2385869

Bulkat, B. A. (2020, June 18). *Car Repossession Laws: An Overview.* Www.Nolo.Com. https://www.nolo.com/legal-encyclopedia/car-repossession-laws-overview.html

Debt Avalanche vs. Debt Snowball: What's the Difference? (n.d.). Investopedia. Retrieved October 2, 2020, from https://www.investopedia.com/articles/personal-finance/080716/debt-avalanche-vs-debt-snowball-which-best-you.asp

Debt Cleanse. (2016, February 11). Kirkus Reviews. https://www.kirkusreviews.com/book-reviews/jorge-p-newbery/debt-cleanse/

Debt Consolidation Loans in UK - Debt Help | Money Advisor. (n.d.). MoneyAdvisor - Here To Help. Retrieved October 2, 2020, from https://www.moneyadvisor.co.uk/debt-plan/debt-consolidation/

Debt Settlement & Negotiating With Creditors. (n.d.). Www.Nolo.Com. Retrieved October 2, 2020, from https://www.nolo.com/legal-encyclopedia/debt-settlement-negotiating-with-creditors

Fay, B. (2014, October 29). *Are Your Student Loans Federal or Private – Do You Know the Difference?* Debt.Org. https://www.debt.org/blog/differences-private-federal-student-loans/

Fay, B. (2017, May 25). *Slaying a $30,000 Student Loan Debt Beast in a Year.* Debt.Org. https://www.debt.org/blog/paying-student-loan-one-year/

George, D. (2019, December 2). *Store Card vs. Traditional Credit Card: What's the Difference?* The Ascent. https://www.fool.com/the-ascent/credit-cards/articles/store-card-traditional-credit-card-whats-difference/

Haden, J. (2020, February 6). *11 Ways to Negotiate Better With Anyone (Especially if You Hate to Negotiate).* Inc.Com. https://www.inc.com/jeff-haden/11-ways-to-negotiate-better-with-anyone-even-if-you-don-t-like-to-negotiate.html

Here's How to Create a Debt Repayment Plan That Truly Does Work. (n.d.). The Balance. Retrieved October 2, 2020, from https://www.thebalance.com/how-to-prioritize-your-debt-repayment-4101918

How the Debt Collection Agency Business Works. (n.d.). Investopedia. Retrieved October 2, 2020, from https://www.investopedia.com/articles/personal-finance/121514/how-debt-collection-agency-business-works.asp

How to Negotiate & Lower Utility Bills - Don't Fret About Debt. (2015, February 3). Don't Fret About Debt. https://www.dontfretaboutdebt.net/negotiate-lower-utility-bills/

Lake, R. (2019, July 23). *What Really Happens if You Default on a Mortgage?* SmartAsset. https://smartasset.com/mortgage/what-really-happens-if-you-default-on-a-mortgage

Leonhardt, M. (2018, August 20). *Here's how much debt Americans have at every age*. CNBC. https://www.cnbc.com/2018/08/20/how-much-debt-americans-have-at-every-age.html

Loftsgordon, A. A. (2020, April 16). *How Judicial Foreclosure Works*. Www.Nolo.Com. https://www.nolo.com/legal-encyclopedia/how-foreclosure-works-30066.html

National Debt. (n.d.). Investopedia. Retrieved October 2, 2020, from https://www.investopedia.com/updates/usa-national-debt/

Overdrafts and Revolving Credit. (2020, February 12). Touch Financial. https://www.touchfinancial.co.uk/finance-options/working-capital-finance/overdrafts-and-revolving-credit/

R. (2017, January 25). *Bankruptcy: How it Works, Types & Consequences*. Experian. https://www.experian.com/blogs/ask-experian/credit-education/bankruptcy-how-it-works-types-and-consequences/

Reiter, M. A. (2012, September 11). *Negotiating With Car Loan Lenders and Car Lease Companies*. Www.Nolo.Com. https://www.nolo.com/legal-encyclopedia/negotiating-with-car-loan-lenders-car-lease-companies.html

Solutions, R. (2020a, June 25). *The Truth About Debt Consolidation*. Daveramsey.Com. https://www.daveramsey.com/blog/debt-consolidation-truth

Solutions, R. (2020b, September 3). *How the Debt Snowball Method Works*. Daveramsey.Com. https://www.daveramsey.com/blog/how-the-debt-snowball-method-works

Steps to Managing Your Debt. (n.d.). The Balance. Retrieved October 2, 2020, from https://www.thebalance.com/how-to-manage-your-debt-960856

Thompson, L. C. A. (2019, December 13). *Damages for FDCPA Violations*. Www.Nolo.Com. https://www.nolo.com/legal-encyclopedia/damages-fdcpa-violations.html

What Does Unsecured Debt Mean? (n.d.). Investopedia. Retrieved October 2, 2020, from https://www.investopedia.com/terms/u/unsecureddebt.asp

What is a Payday Loan? (n.d.). Investopedia. Retrieved October 2, 2020, from https://www.investopedia.com/terms/p/payday-loans.asp

What Is Chapter 7? (n.d.). Investopedia. Retrieved October 2, 2020, from https://www.investopedia.com/terms/c/chapter7.asp

What Is Foreclosure and How Does It Work? (n.d.). The Balance. Retrieved October 2, 2020, from https://www.thebalance.com/foreclosure-explained-315702

What is Payday Lending? (2020, March 9). Stop the Payday Loan Debt Trap. http://stopthedebttrap.org/about/whatispaydaylending/

Your Rights Under the FDCPA: Disputing the Debt. (2019, January 14). New Economy Project. https://www.neweconomynyc.org/your-rights-under-the-fdcpa-disputing-the-debt/

www.ingramcontent.com/pod-product-compliance
Lightning Source LLC
Chambersburg PA
CBHW031632210526
45464CB00004B/1865